I Was Amish

I Was Amish

A personal story of an Amish girl and her life

∞

Malinda Detweiler

Copyright © 2011 by Malinda Detweiler.

Library of Congress Control Number: 2011902528
ISBN: Hardcover   978-1-4568-6990-8
                Softcover   978-1-4568-6989-2
                Ebook   978-1-4568-6991-5

All rights reserved. No part of this book may be reproduced or transmitted in any form or by any means, electronic or mechanical, including photocopying, recording, or by any information storage and retrieval system, without permission in writing from the copyright owner.

Leaving the Amish is not an indictment.

All names and places have been changed for the privacy of everyone in my story

This book was printed in the United States of America.

To order additional copies of this book, contact:
Xlibris Corporation
1-888-795-4274
www.Xlibris.com
Orders@Xlibris.com
93300

Table of Contents

Leaving the Amish 11
The Night I Left 16
A Day like Any Other Day 20
Amish in my Community 27
Church Services in our Community 33
Our Amish Singings 41
The Siblings in Our Family 47
Ramblings of my Play and Friends 58
House of Our Memories 65
The Amish Tyrants 69
Eight Years of School 77
My Sentiments and Distress 84
Years of Turbulence 89
A Secret Breakdown 93
My Starving Sister-in-law 99
The Witch of the Amish Community 108
Times of my Amish Youth 114
Those Bothering Troubles 120
Love and Troubles in a New Environment 126
Dark Moments in Hard Places 133
Many Moves 137
Broken Dream of Love 140
The Many Moves in my Search for Home 145
Consequences of Action 153
Change of Thoughts 162
My Valued Life and Restoration 165

Introduction

WHEN I WAS young, I noticed that many non-Amish people in our community looked at beautiful magazines about the Amish. They watched movies about the Amish, read lovely books, saw large farms and big gardens, visited small Amish tourist towns, and ate delicious home-cooked meals in Amish-advertised restaurants. They were sold the belief that Amish people were honest and hard working. Life was simple and good.

Contrary to the movies, I never saw a barn-raising in our community. I did see a few quilting bees, but never had the patience to learn how to quilt. I never understood why people wanted to do something so slow and boring.

I saw threshing bees as a very young child but they went out of style by the time I was five years old. I worked in Mom's garden and helped her can food. It was such hard work that I vowed never to live like that. I learned how to mend and sew but I decided it was much more fun to buy clothes. I learned how to embroider and wanted to embroider pretty things on my clothes, but Amish culture didn't allow me to do that.

I knew what my own family and community taught me and never believed the perception the rest of the world had of us. I knew their perception was wrong, knowing my own life was not as great as it has been displayed. Just as receiving a glimpse of Germany does not give me a true experience of life there, neither does watching a movie on Amish life reveal an understanding or portray the truth about my Amish life.

People really didn't know, or understand us. I couldn't bear the fact that non-Amish people were so naïve to believe that the lives of Amish people were simple, peaceful, and beautiful. I yearned for them to know the truth and I wanted to be the one to tell them.

Back when I was seventeen years old and living in my Amish community, I longed to stand on rooftops or alongside the road and shout the truth at everyone until my throat hurt and I had nothing left to say. But I couldn't do that back then. I understood the ramifications. Yet I needed to remember my life and reveal the truth. I wrote things down to help me keep that promise.

When I first left my Amish community, I couldn't write things down fast enough. I needed to get it all out of me. The biggest problem with writing meant remembering what happened and reliving everything. As I was stirring up old memories and horrifying experiences, it became necessary for me to relieve the pain of my childhood with alcohol and drugs. Though I no longer wanted to be a sentinel of Amish secrets, the pain I felt urged me to prefer the anonymity of drugs.

Since my recovery, many people have assumed that I became a drug addict in response to my naive Amish upbringing. I disagree. Addicts come from all types of families – rich and poor, alike. From parents who abuse their children, to those who pander to their every need, and from those who neglect their children altogether. People use drugs because they want to escape their horrific surroundings or just because they like the feeling of being high. There are all kinds of people who abuse drugs and a portion of them are Amish.

In my experience, happiness, love, and charity usually came to me when I gave it to others. It's contrary to the counseling which suggests that we give this to ourselves first. I believe that when I gave love and hope only to myself, I lived a lonely life.

My life is not perfect, and I didn't find a happily ever after. I don't yet live in a big house, nor do I have lots of money at this time. I've learned to change things in my life and I'm always striving to make it better. Every effort on my part has paid off. The fog of my life has cleared up and every positive change I've made is a promise of a brighter future.

I accepted life with everything that had inspiration and happiness for me. I learned from counseling, college, drug treatment, and a mending of my thought processes. These good things were used to replace homelessness, drugs, financial disasters and unhappiness. I found stability and respect in my life. I found the other side of misery.

Leaving the Amish

I WAS STANDING in the stillness of the night grasping for comfort and peace in my surroundings. As I stood on a little gravel road which ran behind our house, a foreboding feeling that something terrible would happen flooded my senses. My heart began to pound in the deafening silence as if it was going to implode in terrific destruction. Fear rose within me as I stood on the road, alone and vulnerable.

I began to run from the threatening darkness which frightened me. I knew I had to run to save myself because time was precious and in a moment I could be lost. I would be held in a place of no hope, no redemption, and no relief.

From the darkness a van rolled along filled with people, and in a moment I knew it was the Amish trying to hunt me down. I ran in sheer terror along the dark road as the van sped right along; Amish people trying to grab me, hold me, and keep me.

I desperately wanted to escape capture by the Amish in the van. It was as if a dreadful fate evolved from their trap. Yet they grabbed me, pulled me in, and held me tight. So I blocked out the van, the people; the ride. For a moment my world went blank.

When I opened my eyes I saw people and the dim lights of the van. Expressions of laughter and chatter filled the air as they realized they had me in their clutch now. I looked at the door and saw it was closed tightly. Then their hands reached over and pulled off my clothes, replacing my garments with Amish ones, and the van stopped in the driveway to my home.

Suddenly I saw myself back in my childhood home with my father and mother. The whole family – my brothers, sisters, and both parents – stood in front of me, watching me as if I were a prisoner.

I sat in a soft chair in the corner of the living room while gazes ready to erupt in rage stared at me from every direction. I sat on the chair as if glued, looking for an escape but finding none. Now I realized I was trapped and couldn't move.

Weeks passed with no outlet, no relief. I was desperate because time had stopped, frozen in place. Blackness enveloped me as I realized that the worst had just happened and now it was too late.

What a chilling dream!

Suddenly the sun was shining in my eyes as I lay on the grass in the yard by the side of the house where I had dropped, crying. It took me a moment to realize I must have fallen asleep and just had another nightmare. Complete relief swept over me as I arose, still sweaty and disoriented, and with trembling legs looked for water to drink. Hesitating for just a moment to regain my senses, I gazed across the lawn and admired the beautiful green grass and the yellow dandelions. I noticed the little black calf in our back pasture and the roughly hewn house he went to for protection and feed. I listened to the sound of the freight train in the distance. I knew I still had time, time to escape and make it right. I headed to the kitchen for water.

* * *

The first time my family discovered I was interested in leaving Amish life was on a Saturday. Eighteen year old Teresa, my sister, and I were in the kitchen preparing food. I was seventeen. My heart fell because I knew she wouldn't like what I had to say. Yet, I told her anyway because I felt the truth was required of me, a submission to the Amish.

We were standing across from one another, talking across the table. My heart began to pound as I thought about what I should tell her. She gave me that opportunity when she said, "Mom and Dad want you to get baptized on Sunday and everyone your age is doing it."

I said, "I don't know if I want to get baptized."

Puzzled, she asked, "Why not?"

"Perhaps I want to leave the Amish," I said.

She stared at me for a moment, "You know you can't change your mind once you're baptized."

I said, "Then I should wait to get baptized until I know for certain."

She raised her voice, saying, "No, you need to get baptized rather than thinking and making the wrong choice."

I replied, "What if it's the wrong choice for me to be Amish?"

She was shouting now. "The Bible makes it clear that we have to be Amish, it's evil to own cars, it makes you worldly, and it's evil to forsake Amish clothes!"

Teresa began to pressure me with oodles of questions about religion. Tension and emotional friction rose in the kitchen. It was hard for me to answer her questions with our differences at hand. Today I could easily answer the questions and put Teresa in the same discomfort she gave me. Back then she didn't give me a chance to think clearly. The Amish as I knew them are gifted in turning any controversial issue backwards or upside down and Teresa was no exception.

I didn't agree with her and it was no use arguing. She had a way of defending all things Amish, even inconsistencies. I regretted telling Teresa the truth and more than ever I wished for courage to stand up to her. After all I found it miserable to put up with her harassment. However I knew that people who leave the Amish get harassed by those believing it's their religious duty to bring you back.

Teresa ran outside to tell Mom and Dad the shocking news about my intended apostasy. Mom and Dad were agitated and quick to respond. They were sure I would change my mind if I became a church member. They decided I had an emotional disorder as most Amish people assume when someone wants to leave. They were sure I wouldn't leave the Amish if I were emotionally healed by visiting a counselor. They also saw me as a person who was hell bound if I were to leave.

This "counselor" is someone in which actually, Amish have zero professional training in. This was also a counselor who didn't have a clue what we faced.

I decided it was better not to argue with my family. I was afraid of the vengeance that would target me. Furthermore, I had a need to hide from anger and hostility. In my world I had already seen too much of it.

We had freedom of choice to leave the Amish without being shunned if we weren't a church member. In fact we could experiment in two different worlds. For example, noncompliant youth (teenagers) would participate in wild and rebellious "worldly" parties to experiment the other "side of the fence". The decent and compliant Amish youth had "singings" to show their contentedness. Sometimes the wilder youth would attend with the compliant youth at singings, but later would wander out into the yard during the activities and behave in rebellious ways. Yet those "wild" actions certainly didn't seem to persuade youth to leave. Furthermore the youth weren't necessarily condoned if they left.

Furthermore I knew I wanted to leave the Amish despite it being the wrong time for me to leave. I certainly didn't need a raging drunken experience to show me the way to the other side of the fence. Such a way of thinking was senseless to me.

Putting aside the way that youth were brought up, I had to deal with another issue and that was shunning. The complete and total freedom to leave was forbidden.

This is because Amish people shun those who are baptized church members and than fail to follow the *Ordnung*. Therefore I didn't want to be a baptized church member and endure shunning when I left. Rather I preferred not to become a church member so I could leave later, without the shunning.

Member or not, it really didn't matter. The pressure was on to get baptized and receive peace from the Amish or suffer their animosity while I waited. Now I knew I wouldn't be able to leave home by morning. It was Sunday tomorrow, and something must happen to keep the peace. I remained quiet, wordlessly quiet. "Quiet" was contained in the performance of an unwanted baptism, hushing my parents with action.

I realized that the Amish view the baptism as something serious and life-binding. Anyone who leaves after being baptized is literally "dead" in there eyes. I suppose that may be Amish peoples' view of me. Yet I had already experienced what it felt like to be condemned to the level which made me afraid to choose what I wanted. Now I did something of their choosing rather than mine, the baptismal.

On Sunday the bishop sprinkled water on my head in a ceremony of baptism. He recited some High German passages which I didn't understand, (our understanding of High German is not taught in the level in which they preach), but I knew they were associated with a vow to stay Amish because that was explained to me by my siblings. I didn't believe in that vow so I decided the vow didn't matter. In my heart I wasn't a church member. I was simply avoiding animosity from Amish people.

I stress that I didn't want to leave for reasons of hate and rebellion. It was just that to remain Amish meant that I had to wear what the Old Order Amish Mennonite church dictated. I had to eat what Dad decreed and like what Mom decided for me. I had to accept all Amish religious requirements. To accept the Amish way would control me, forcing me to live by standards other than my own. I wanted to think for myself, decide things for myself, and not let others control me.

I also had a different religious perspective from the Amish. For example, I disagreed with the Amish people for prohibiting freedom, passing down tradition and ritual relentlessly to the next generation. I disagreed with an *Ordnung* that defied common sense. I disagreed with their judgment upon those who choose to leave and the baptismal vow. I disagreed with the pressure they heap on insiders to remain within the culture.

The Amish church excommunicated others when they left and I knew they would also excommunicate me when I left. I had to come to terms with that.

In doing so, I stoically believe I should respect my Amish family as much as possible with our differences at hand, completely forgiving their practice of shunning which they see as an act of love.

I had known as early as the age of seventeen that I would leave the Amish someday. This was after I read many books smuggled in from the library in my special retreat in the quiet of the attic. The books inspired me to seek change and happiness. It gave me ideas and aspirations.

I also wanted to survive and be happy. In order for me to survive I had to throw away my fears and leave. I did this at age twenty, several years after I knew I would leave.

In light of all this, I slipped off into the night and left my childhood home forever. Entering a new world, I left a bushel of heartaches behind me, never knowing the troubles that lay ahead.

The Night I Left

IT WAS THE last night in August. It was also a warm, beautiful summer night. I was leaving home the only way I believed would be successful. I tried to open a window and changed my mind. It made too much noise. I packed my belongings and silently carried them past my parents' open bedroom door while they slept. I took off my shoes and left my socks on. I didn't want to wake anyone.

I moved all my things outside and looked for a place to hide them. I picked up two packages and started taking them to an old forsaken building. I thought it would be safe to leave my things there until I'd be able to get them later.

Our white Eskimo dog named, Fluffy started barking non-stop and I was sure that Dad would come outside to check on him. I knew that if I wanted to leave, I should go now. I panicked and ran down the street before anyone saw me. I ran until I was out of sight.

I was in my socks on a gravel road wearing a fanny pack with fifty dollars in it. I earned the money from working in Mom's bakery. I also had a writing tablet tucked in my fanny pack that had some of my life history on it. I walked fast for two miles on the gravel road and then I discovered my socks were torn. I took off my socks and kept switching between running and walking barefoot.

I knew it was not safe on the street, all alone. I jumped into the ditch whenever a car came driving past just for safety. I hid in the ditch until the traffic passed and then continued my travel.

I reached a nearby town around midnight. I stood behind the small hardware store, thinking about my next move. I took the time to let my hair down and brush it out.

I knew I needed to run and jump. I gathered each side of my blouse, pulled it together toward the center, and knotted it. I gathered my skirt by the waistband where it hung open, tugged vigorously, and pulled it together, knotting that as well. The material was stretchy, which made the knotting easy.

I thought about staying with a girl that lived in our community. She had left the Amish a few months earlier and still lived in town. I changed my mind after realizing that I didn't know her well and the only thing I really knew about her was that her dad had sexually abused her as a child. I didn't know where else to go except to my (brother, Ray's wife) sister-in-law, Ann's old counselor. I decided to go there believing it to be a better choice.

I continued walking and running to the town where Ann's counselor lived. I made it to the furthest reaches of the Amish community by early morning. I was lying in the ditch waiting for traffic to pass when a vehicle stopped. It was very close to where I was hiding. Several men vacated the vehicle and searched the weeds just a few yards from me. I lay low in the ditch and held my breath, waiting. After searching through the weeds, the men left.

With relief I continued my journey only to realize that my feet had big blisters by now, and I was sore and limping. I started looking around for help. I finally saw a house as I walked along so I picked up my courage and knocked on the door. A woman answered the door and I asked her if I could call a taxi.

She was rude and bluntly asked me if I were a runaway. She told me she didn't know anything about taxis. Her large dog growled at me and I was terrified. I didn't let it show but simply smiled at the rude woman, talking kindly to her dog. This seemed to charm her and I left without a problem.

I finally reached another small town and three large dogs greeted me with hostility. The dogs came charging out of the woods, snarling and showing their teeth. I fled for the nearest building and made it inside. The dogs guarded the door growling whenever I looked outside.

I realized that the dogs had me trapped inside the building now. So I sat on a chair flipping through a magazine while waiting for the dogs to leave, but they wouldn't go. I decided to investigate the building while I waited. I looked at all the antiques lying around and while doing so I found a key in the back door. I proceeded to unlock this door, but then I noticed that the dogs came to guard the back door, too! I went back to the front door and waited for the dogs to leave. The dogs finally quieted down and I sneaked through the back door, unseen.

I crept at a low position through a field and got back to the road again. I found myself standing at a crossroad, thinking about which way I should go. A large, black dog stood sentinel across one of the streets so I knew I wouldn't go in that direction. He was so large that he covered most of the road. I hadn't seen a large dog like that before. He held still without ever moving. So I went through the other road and continued my travel.

It became increasingly difficult to walk as I went along. My blisters doubled in size and filled with blood. As I kept walking I noticed a car stop next to me. A gracious woman with her little girl stopped and offered me a ride and I accepted with relief. The woman told me she noticed I had been walking for a long time. She dropped me off in a little town and I proceeded to look for Jacob, Ann's old counselor.

Jacob didn't seem to be there anymore. I asked people if they had seen him anywhere. Nobody seemed to know him. I decided that I needed to stay at a preacher or a counselor's house while in unfamiliar territory. I thought I might have a better chance for safety.

Call me crazy and endangered for walking straight up to a strange place and looking for a place to live; yeah, that is crazy and possibly even dangerous. On the other side of the coin, I thought I had nothing to lose. After all, I had already been affected by every level of abuse in my childhood home and the Amish community where I was raised. I was willing to take my risks in order to see the other side of life.

Putting aside my conversations of risk taking, I saw a church on the corner of the street and decided to check it out. I went to the house next to the church and knocked on the door. An elderly woman named Penny came to the door and invited me inside. I started crying as I told her my situation. She told me I might like it in her church, and I should stay.

Penny questioned my age saying I looked like a thirteen year old run-away. I convinced her that I was twenty years old, my actual age. She showed me the bathroom and brought me some towels. I took a shower and put on a dress that Penny laid out for me. She had talked to her husband, Bob, while I was taking my shower. When I came back downstairs, she told me I could stay and they would help me find a place of my own and a job.

They called me their daughter and said they were my new parents. They claimed that they were like Abraham and Sarah because they became parents in old age. I was at my first place, about to start a new life and I wondered what lay ahead of me. I was scared, I had sore feet, but I was ready for new adventures, glad to take risks and learn new things.

I was especially glad to be free from my childhood and the burden of its control.

A Day like Any Other Day

I STOOD BREATHLESS *in the garden on a warm sunny afternoon. Tugging at my blue cotton dress, I hurriedly pulled my sleeves up and crossed my arms in an effort to close out the presence of pain that was surrounding me. Squatting down between the long rows of corn, I placed my hand on the one inch collar sewn to my dress, wondering why it had to be measured exactly to an inch. I brushed stray hair from my eyes and brushed my hair with my hand where it was parted exactly in the center of my head, as Amish ladies do. I had it pulled back tightly on each side and tied up in the back with plain black hairpins and bobby pins. I had a red kerchief pinned to my hair. I tried my best to become a caterpillar in my handmade cocoon – to insulate myself from the harshness that surrounded me.*

Father was beating Teresa and he had been doing it for a long time. He had pulled up her dress and pulled down her panties for the beating. I wanted to yell, "Stop, Dad, stop! You're hurting her!" but I didn't dare. I wanted to scream and beat on his back but I knew the uncontrollable rage of Father. I would be his next victim if I dared to protest his cruelty and I was afraid of him.

Dad kept on pounding Teresa's bare bottom without restraint or mercy, not listening to her pleas for mercy or her uncontrollable cries. My older brothers and sisters silently stared at Father, everyone much too frightened to defend her. His eyes were bloodshot, his forehead furled. He stared at me, pounding his fist against her face and thighs. I couldn't look my father in the eye. He surely would have beaten me if I challenged him even in the slightest way.

"She will never defy the Amish now! Forget God, but we can't bring the Amish to shame," he said proudly. "See, it hurt her for the good of the Amish." He pointed at the crumpled, trembling Teresa. My brothers and sisters gasped just like me, but they turned away from Dad and cast their gaze downward. They knew better than to question Dad's methods, because they had already learned this lesson.

Teresa lay on the ground, gasping for air. She tried to say something in a weak stutter for help but she could only muster a gurgle. Just one little cry before she grew silent altogether.

"See there," he nodded toward Teresa "it didn't hurt her one bit. Tell her I did it especially for the cause of decent Amish."

"Yes Dad." My eyes welled up and tears spilled out onto my cheeks as I bent over to shield Teresa as much as possible while I helped her pull her panties up. I turned just a bit so that my back was to Dad. I was certain crying wasn't going to help my case, nor was it my intent. I felt so sad that she had been hurt for the cause of the Amish.

I stifled my sobs as I walked fearfully to the house with Teresa but the tears kept flowing. I buried my face into my blue cotton dress. It was still warm and sticky. It seemed fair – my tears, for the Amish religion and all its goodness.

"Der, der, that's enough crying for you," Mother said when I reached the house.

"Yes, Mom" I said. I looked up at Mother, my face ruddy with tears "Dad says he did it especially for the Amish."

"Go wash up and change your clothes before your father sees you." Mother turned and walked away in an irritated manner. I walked to my bedroom and hid behind the door until bedtime.

It is difficult to describe my earliest childhood memories as many are dim in my mind. My earliest recollection is of my father beating me.

"Stop hitting her. She doesn't understand," my mother would say from behind the wood-burning stove in our living room.

"Yes, she does." Father continued hitting me across my bare lower back and buttocks.

"No. She doesn't know why you're doing this," Mother set her jaw and tightened her lips. She even raised her voice just a tad without actually shouting. The tremor in her voice was unmistakable, and all the while, she stood with the wood-burning stove as a barrier between her and my father.

"She'll learn! By the time I'm done with her, she'll know."

Of course, I didn't know what I did that deserved such a beating. Dad never said. This, however, was typical for Dad. He never told us what was bad and what wasn't. Then again, most of the time, we hadn't done anything particularly bad or even wrong.

* * *

I heard my mother singing in the kitchen. She had a lovely voice. Unfortunately, I failed to hear its beauty at the 4 a.m. wake-up call. Early as this morning was, I was a bit grateful to wake from my dreaming. Yet I was also grouchy and very tired.

It was dark, but I was not lighting a kerosene lamp. It took time and was tedious at 4:00 a.m. I opened my bedroom door to let some light shine in from the rest of the house so I could get dressed.

I could wear either a green dress or a brown one for my day attire. Both dresses were equally ugly and practical cotton dresses for school, suitable for any season. I decided on the one-piece, green dress. I put small straight pins in the front of my blouse and waist to close it. Amish girls in our community may not wear buttons on their clothing once they become preadolescent or older and I was preadolescent.

I went into the kitchen for breakfast. Mom had cooked a heavy breakfast as usual. A typical Amish tradition in our home was to serve a hearty meal whenever our family ate together. This morning Mom fixed scrambled eggs with melted cheese, toast, bacon and oatmeal.

As usual Father reached for his spoon. He waited until he thought Mother wasn't looking and reached across the table for the sugar bowl. Mother surprised him, holding fast to the spoon in his hand.

"Let go of my hand, Mother. I am perfectly capable of sweetening my own oatmeal."

"Now, Father, you use way too much sugar. You don't need three spoonfuls of it. It's not good for your health."

"I know my age. And I know better than you what I like to eat." He tugged half-heartedly at his spoon hand and then quickly poured the sugar over his oatmeal straight from the sugar bowl.

This was a typical argument for Dad and Mom. Dad won most of the time, at which we all sighed a breath of relief. When Mom won, we held our breaths just a little longer and tip-toed whenever we drew near Dad. I tried to ignore their disputes whenever I could. I figured, why fuss over something like sugar on Dad's oatmeal? It ultimately made no difference. Eventually, Dad would eat his oatmeal the way he wanted. On the other hand, we kids always paid the price for Mom's victories.

After breakfast, Father sat at the table and lectured my brothers on the chores he wanted them to do. He talked incessantly, specifically detailing each chore. Breakfast was never really over without a lecture from my father.

After the lecture my brothers went outside to do their chores and Dad sat and stared at us girls. After a long stare-down, he sat in his recliner and read his High German Bible. He was the deacon of our Old Order Amish Mennonite Church. He had to practice his High German.

I went back to my room and finished getting ready for school. I disliked going to school but I went anyway. I walked the old, muddy, dirt road to school with my sisters. I was glad when I came to the end of the dirt road and walked on paved streets. I didn't enjoy the long walk but I would rather stay on that road than be at school.

My dread grew inside me during recess because everyone played baseball. So I went inside to work on my math problems instead. I hated math above all subjects, but I preferred it to a game of baseball. Math and baseball were two things that I was not gifted in and they were two things that were very popular in our school.

I stayed late after school to finish my schoolwork. Our teachers did not believe in much homework so we had to finish everything in class or stay after school to finish it. We had chores to do at home, which were considered more important.

I took my time walking home from school. In the morning, the walk on the way to school was long and tiresome, but in the afternoon, the road was never long enough. I wanted to get home later rather than sooner because I wasn't excited about doing my chores.

That evening, Mom fixed bread soup for supper. She set the food on the table so everyone could help themselves as she often did. We didn't necessarily have to eat together as a family and tonight was no exception. I took one look at the soggy bread soaked in milk and decided to fix a different supper for myself.

I got the salt shaker, a paring knife, and a slice of bread from the pantry and spread mayonnaise on my bread. I went behind the house where wood tables were set up, spread full of fresh tomatoes from the garden. I peeled and sliced a tomato and fixed a tomato sandwich for myself. I was grateful for the freedom to eat alone and relaxed as I watched the sun set from across the field.

My sister Darlene and I washed the dishes after everyone finished eating. Every day after school we carried firewood to the house from the woodshed. Our last chore was to gather the eggs from the henhouse and let the hens out of their coops.

I went to the desk to read a book before I went to bed. The books in my desk were read many times. My parents did not know the prize they gave me in books. Books mesmerized me. I read a variety of them, from "Joni" by Joni Tada Erickson to "The Hiding Place" by Corrie ten Boom. I read "Runaway to Freedom" and "Dorie, the Girl Nobody Loved". I loved "Little Women" and "Little House on the Prairie". When I ran out of books, I read every magazine I could find. My books were my best friends.

Not all of my memories were sad. For example, we often played peek-around the corner – a game where we ran around the house, always trying to hide, walking, or moving from the seeker. If the seeker caught us then we became the seeker.

In the summer, we entertained ourselves until the cool breeze of the evening surrounded us. The locusts sang and an aura of enchantment filled the air. I felt the cool breeze on my feet (we were always barefoot during the summer) and knew that night was on its way.

When it was dark outside, we caught fireflies until late in the evening. We pulled the lights from the fireflies' little tails and stuck the lights to our forehead. Then we watched the lightless bugs fly away.

When we were older, we went camping one weekend in the summertime. I remember the long trip as I pushed the wheelbarrow full of camping gear to the woods. When we arrived at our campsite, we laid out our blankets and rested. We fixed our campfire and listened to the howl of the coyote as we lay on the bumpy ground.

The next morning we headed toward the waterfall. We sat underneath the rushing water and let it splash on us. Then we ran up to the large rock that emerged over the waterfall to lie down and soak in the summer. We also walked through the creek bed and looked for sharp, black rocks. They served as chalk, and were perfect for writing on the big white rocks. When the weekend was over, we complained all the way home because we didn't want to go back to normal life.

As for me, I lived in my own fantasies. I imagined little milkmaids bringing the cows' home from the pasture. I imagined an enchanted forest with fairy creatures and read enchanted books. Perhaps I saved my mind for another world. It was much more pleasant than the real world; better than my father's temper and my mother's nervous flustering. In my own imagination, I was in a happy place.

Dear Journal,

Why can't girls have buttons like boys do? I hate pinning my dress every morning. They itch and poke and prick me, sometimes they even make me bleed. I would say it's like torture but compared to Dad's punishment, it's not that painful but it's really, annoying.

Dad beat me again today. I wish I knew what I did wrong. Emma says we must watch ourselves when Dad is around and to do <u>exactly</u> as he says. I tried. I really did. But I feel like it doesn't matter what I do or how I do it. I get beat anyways - just for breathing.

Dad says, even if he beat me for something I said I didn't do, The Amish would eventually know the truth and it would bring them shame. "You can't lie to them." If that's true, and I'm guessing it is, since the one thing Dad truly knows is about the Amish. I know that is supposed to be good and biblical and God surely approves it. Yet I dream of living in a better place, one that lets girls wear buttons on their dresses. I want a place that is happy all the time and where nobody gets hurt. If that place does exist, I think fairies would live there.

Is it possible that fairies are real, Journal? I think they would live by the waterfall - you know the one where we went camping. I think they would use the lights of lightning bugs for their lanterns and the caps of little acorns would be their basins. They could use the basins to wash their little hands and faces. Wouldn't that be something? I mean, if they did exist, I would want to shrink myself down to their size and live with them forever. But if they don't exist, I will find someplace else to live other than here. When I'm old enough . . . anywhere else would be better. It has to be, right?

Well, Journal, that was my day in a nutshell. Until next time.

                                          Forever and always, Regina

Amish in my Community

I WAS RAISED in the Old Order Amish Church. Amish is a religion in the same way that Christianity, Islam, and Judaism are religions. There are so many varieties of Mennonites and Amish around the world that I cannot possibly cover the many shades of belief or practice among them.

"Adherence to the *Ordnung* varies among families and church districts."[1] In light of this knowledge, my book can only reflect my personal experiences in my community, yet in some instances, others have explained what I have lived.

"The Amish stem from Swiss Anabaptists who emerged during the Protestant Reformation in sixteenth-century Europe. The Amish emerged as a distinctive group in 1693, following a rift within the Anabaptist family that led to Amish and Mennonite factions.

The Amish were named for Jakob Ammann, A Swiss-born elder, who played a central role in the schism that tore the Swiss and South German Anabaptists asunder in the 1690s. Despite several differences, the contention over shunning drove the decisive wedge between Ammann's followers and the established Swiss leaders.

---

[1] Donald Kraybill, "The Quiet Spirit," pp. 13 and 14.

Various Mennonite groups, scattered around the globe, also trace their lineage to the Radical Reformation. They take their name from Menno Simons, a Dutch priest, who converted to Anabaptism in 1536 and became an influential preacher and writer.

Between 1536 and 1600s thousands of Anabaptist lost their heads to the executioner's sword, died in prison, burned at the stake, drowned in rivers, and endured innumerable forms of torture for their religious faith. The story of this bloody theater is recorded in the 1,200-page Martyrs Mirror. Martyrs Mirror is often found in Amish homes to keep the memories of persecution fresh among the Amish today."[2]

I knew, as most people know, that Old Order Amish mostly live in Pennsylvania and Ohio. Although most Amish live there, I didn't grow up there. I grew up in a small Amish community in Missouri. We had names for some additional sects, not for others.

I saw a few "Beachy" Amish as an Amish child. I was fascinated to see Old Order Amish who could own a car as long as the car is black, speak English, and still dress Amish. We had Beachy Amish friends and therefore had reason to visit them. Therefore we remained casual and had infrequent conversations with them.

We had Amish relatives who lived in Lagrange, Indiana and also in Minnesota. They had electricity but still dressed Amish and were Old Order Amish like us. We thought they were fancy, and some Amish people in our community disapproved of them.

My sisters and I complained greatly about communities where men could have modern appliances to farm and the women weren't allowed to have modern appliances at all. A few small communities like these existed. My youngest brother Lamar went to visit one of them and we talked about the *Ordnung* for months after that.

From my experience, every state that has Amish communities has two varieties of communities. Usually, one community is rather modern and one is extremely old-fashioned. I remember when my youngest brother, Lamar, went to visit a community in Minnesota to see if he wanted to move there. He was disgusted when the church service was dismissed and all the Amish men went behind the barn to smoke tobacco pipes. Although Lamar liked the plain community, he wouldn't move to a place where people smoked.

---

[2] Donald Kraybill, "The Riddle of Amish Culture", p. 114

We didn't have equal income in our community or in any community. I saw some Amish who were rather wealthy and others quite poor and the rest were somewhere in-between.

When I went to the Farmer's Market in Kansas City with Mom I saw German Baptists and brethren of other Mennonite religions selling their wares. They were more modern than we were. Yet I knew this wasn't true about all Mennonites. Some Mennonites are stricter than other Amish – all depending on their choice of rules, their *Ordnung*. Amish people shun their church brethren for leaving the Amish to become Mennonite. They disagree with Mennonites for the difference in rules and religious opinions. Our community certainly did.

There were several things I didn't know. For example, I was taught that all non-Amish people were secular, liberal minded moderns. We were the Amish church separate from the world. Therefore we were the good and they were the bad. We barely knew the difference between a religious or non-religious outsider. Anyone who wasn't Amish was a liberal, which meant they were modern and worldly.

We had company from time to time from New Order Amish people. They were more spiritual than we were and believed in being Christians personally with Christ. They believed their destiny was to convert Old Order Amish people like us to Christ. They didn't shun me when I left the Amish, and in fact accepted me as long as I believed in Christianity. However, they believed that the conversion to Christ was more acceptable if I dressed Amish because Amish people would accept me better in plain clothes.

Therefore they still believe one must be Amish in order to be of true Christian value. They still adhere harshly to an Amish style of living and have the attitude that people need condemnation when they leave them. On the other hand, Old Order Amish people in our community shun New Order Amish for the difference in religion.

Old Order Amish people are more or less mere believers in the religious traditions and lifestyle of the Amish, which they believe to be godly. They believe the submission to the *Ordnung* is a godly ordering of their life.

When I left the Amish I was well aware that I would be shunned. I had watched several of my aunts and their families leave the Amish. I had listened to the grievance of my parents as they talked about my aunts. I knew that Amish people strictly forbid people to eat or exchange things with ex-communicated people.

If we found out that someone in our community left the Amish my mother would say, "The person knew the Bible too well." This meant the person read the Bible too much and became too intelligent. Therefore, they could outsmart others with their biblical knowledge and make the case that it was right to leave the Amish.

One time a secular man came to our community to become Amish. He came to church frequently and made an effort to be accepted, but the bishop told Dad to make the man leave. Amish children mocked the man and people stared at him. He was not accepted and he was also not treated kindly.

Dad would say, "He can't come to our world and we are evil if we go to his world." He'd also say, "It's important to do what our parents raised us to do." It did not matter if the way our parents raised us was senseless. I saw evidence that the Amish pass judgments on those who leave to become outsiders or those who try to become insiders.

In our community ten years seems to be the given time for forgiveness or acceptance of those who resisted their *Ordnung*. Relationships with the shunned people could be mended after ten year of leaving the Amish family and community. Ten years passed after I left the Amish when my own Amish family started connecting to me in a manner of acceptance. My aunt left the Amish and the first tolerated visit with her parents, my grandparents, was after ten years.

Amish people, like those in our community and most Amish communities, have rules that do not let Amish people own cars. The Amish usually, but not always, believe the forgiveness process starts after the person sells the car and it is no longer in their possession. In our community a person was required to make church confessions to the bishop for ten years after he sold his car.

I believe it is an act of hypocrisy to forbid cars, but then pay non-Amish drivers for transportation.

Amish people in our community were taught to read and spell, to a certain degree, in High German. We learned this in school as children. We didn't know how to speak nor did we learn vocabulary in High German. We spoke some Dutch but didn't read, write, or spell it. Neither language is known fluently. The mother tongue of Amish people is a Dutch German dialect, but a lot of English is mixed in. Most people refer to it as Pennsylvania Dutch. Although I have met Amish relatives who speak a more fluent Dutch dialect, it was difficult for me to understand them.

Amish people in our community were forbidden to use the law such as the police or fire department to stop illegal practices. To call the police would bring an onslaught of judgment and harassment from Amish people.

If people in our community did something against the *Ordnung*, the offender was required to make a public church confession. It was a recited High German prayer to the bishop while kneeling before him. Both men and women make these recited confessions, only church members. The distinction between church and community member is baptism.

Through some of these confessions I learned about the horror of bestiality in our community. Of course, petty confessions often followed, such as listening to music or wearing bobby pins that weren't darkly colored. I never heard about a confession where someone admitted to physical abuse. Yet I heard many stories throughout the community of women, little girls, and boys being physically and sexually abused and it appeared to be an epidemic in our community.

Perhaps abuse among the Amish isn't worse than any other place in the world, but I know we had far less protection. The bishop had the responsibility to protect the victims, but he was just as likely to shun anyone who reported abuse. I listened to many stories where he refused to help Amish people who came to him. It was this lack of protection that made me want to leave the Amish.

I met some Amish people that took advantage of others in business. They were dishonest, untrustworthy people. I knew that good and bad people existed, regardless of religion. I knew my beginnings and where I grew up, which taught me lessons in my heart. And I knew one thing, above all else – the abuse of little children – the abuse I received when I was a child – was wrong.

It became increasingly more difficult in our community to be financially productive as a farmer. Therefore the Amish in our community became involved with commercial business not related to farming. In our community we owned businesses such as bakeries, stores, and restaurants while advertising to tourists.

Tourism helped me become aware of the discordance between the picture of what Amish life looked like and what I had to endure in reality. I became aware that the tourists had many misconceptions about our personal lives, viewing us as close-knit families with great love for each other. They never realized that we had ugly, dirty problems within our community and family, and how hard it was to follow the *Ordnung* in our daily lives, even to the pressed and specific clothing we wore to church. It was the admiration of the tourists that made me realize, I needed to tell the truth and tell my story.

When tourists took pictures of us Amish, they wondered why we Amish were so hostile. We believed on the second commandment, Exodus 20:4 and in fact heard of it in numerous church services, "Thou shalt not make unto thee any graven image, or any likeness of anything that is in heaven above, or that is in the earth beneath, or that is in the water under the earth." We believed a picture of a person is a graven image and created pride. Certainly I was taught that concept.

I disagree that Amish are independents as the tourists believed we were, because in our community we were not allowed to have a phone so we constantly used the neighbor's phone to make calls. Some Amish people in our community owned cell phones, but they were considered to be rebellious, and we talked against them.

In our community we were taught not to have modern conveniences, but in a way we had them anyway. We had refrigerators, bathrooms, fans, and bright lights. Large car batteries with power jacks and powerful volts, generators with high powered air drill hoses and charges gave us the same power as those who used electricity. We had some modern technology but chose it at a different pace.

While there are many different sects of Amish, my focus is based on the experiences in the community in which I grew up, which is full of hypocrisy – especially with respect to the stance on electricity and treatment of women, children and animals. Additionally, while the Amish are often seen by tourists as independent from the outside world, they're always depending on neighbors for car rides, phone calls, etc.

Church Services in our Community

AMISH PEOPLE IN our community had church twice a month on Sundays. It lasted three hours with families taking turns having church in there home. We sat on hard, backless benches which were delivered in an enclosed bench wagon.

My mother wore her specific clothes for church such as her white organdy cape, apron and head covering, as all Amish women do. She also wore a black shawl and bonnet when it got cold on church Sundays. She fastened her clothes with small, straight pins at all times.

I wore a "monly," a mini shawl with buttons and a bonnet to church. I also wore a white, organdy apron and black organdy head covering in church. I fastened all my clothes with buttons as all little girls did. We could wear any color dress except white, pink or yellow.

Dad wore a white shirt and a black suit to church as all men did in our community. He fastened his suit with hooks and eyes, using buttons otherwise. He also wore a beard and a black felt hat, a vest and coat to church. My brothers wore a white shirt and black pants in church, fastening everything with buttons.

Once we were dressed we would drive to church in our surrey, (two seated buggy). Dad would drive and Mom would sit next to him. We kids sat in the back seat with a heavy blanket across our lap. We hoped the horse wouldn't get frightened and shy away from something whereas Dad would beat the horse.

When we got to church we all stood quietly lined up on a porch or entryway with our arms folded across our chest, waiting. Everyone who was a church member would shake hands with all others in the room. Elders would kiss each other once on the cheek as a sign of respect and to obey scripture. In single line file we'd enter the church and sit.

The elders started church by singing High German songs. They sang the songs very slowly, singing one word in the same amount of time that I could sing an entire large paragraph. The first song is always different, but the second song is always the same song.

The church elders (bishop, preachers and deacon) always leave to go to a different location close to the church when everyone starts singing the second song. They leave to have their own private council. They return when everyone finishes singing the second song, lasting for thirty minutes.

I don't know what the Amish elders discuss in thirty minutes. I know they always take people with them who are supposed to make church confessions to the bishop. They discuss rules they want to enforce and say many things in High German that are too hard to understand. Honestly, no one knows exactly what they discuss.

We started our usual High German sermon after the singing and elder council is over. One scripture often quoted in our Amish church services was, "Be not conformed to this world, but be transformed by the renewing of your mind that ye may prove what is good and acceptable and the perfect will of God" (Romans 12:2). We were admonished to be different from the world and we were different in dress and lifestyle. I believe our mind and behavior should also be separate from the world, unlike them.

"The dimensions of our Amish religion rested on the *Gelassenheit*, (a German word),[3] a blueprint of the *Gelassenheit*. "The personality it taught us to live by were a respect toward behaving reserved, modest, calm and quiet. The symbols we portrayed were, dress, horse, carriage and dialect. Values we carried were submission, obedience, humility

---

[3] Donald Kraybill, "The Riddle of Amish Culture," on page 31

and simplicity. The rituals we practiced were kneeling, foot washing, confession and shunning."

The church services we had were long, tedious, and hard to understand. We didn't know High German well and the sermon became a monotone chant, with many condemnations of hell slurred into it. Many people slept through the church service and many babies cried. Sometimes a child got spanked during church service, stirring the tension in our nerves.

I remember when Lenora, Lamar, and the Bishop's daughter Mary had their baptismal at church. They knelt before the Bishop while he recited various biblical passages.

The Bishop's wife wanted to watch the baptismal and she couldn't see it from where she sat because Dora's (my best friend) grandmother had innocently sat in her seat. She asked Dora's grandmother to move to a different location in the church so she could take her place to watch the baptismal. Dora's grandmother refused to move. She said, "I won't miss out on a baptismal since I came all this way to church." The Bishop's wife was clearly perturbed but she went back to her previous seat and missed out on her own daughter's baptismal.

Furthermore I remember sitting in front of the Bishop when I was seventeen years old. He would talk to me, trying to prepare me to be Amish. Most of the things he said were inconsistent and difficult to understand. It meant nothing to me to be spoken to in a High German language, which I was not taught well. It served as a barrier between us.

I submissively and ignorantly agreed to everything he said. I didn't ask any questions in an effort to avoid conflict. Only one thing the Bishop said was clearly specified. He said that all facts of abuse were to stay inside the Amish church. The message was hypocritical, conflicting and confusing. Yet I determined within myself that someday I would reveal the truth.

Once a year, the Amish in our community have a council meeting service. It is a service that must be done before communion every year. The service can take all day and often it does.

Every one takes turns breaking for lunch in the middle of the service because the service is very lengthy. The same lunch is served that you would find at other church services. The lunch consists of beets, pickles and sandwich spreads. The sandwich spreads are peanut butter mixes, egg and ham salads, cheese spreads, and jelly. They also serve hot drinks such as coffee and tea.

When council meeting church service is resumed the bishop goes over a long list of *Ordnung* rules which we are to follow. The rules will be anything including don't own television sets, don't own cars, this is what the width of the seams in the shirts and dresses must be, this is how the reflectors must look on the buggy's, etc.

Many insignificant, even valueless rules are made. After all they believed we have to be Amish to reach heaven and Amish people must have Amish rules to enforce humility and separateness from the world. The rules were whatever the Bishop decided it is and we had to show our submission by being obedient to it.

"The Amish blueprint 'rules' for expected behavior is called the *Ordnung*. (*Ordnung d*oesn't translate readily into the English language)." A council meeting service is an *Ordnung* church and the different rules' the Bishop speaks of is the *Ordnung*.

"It is sometimes rendered as discipline. The *Ordnung* is best thought of as an ordering of the whole way of life. A code of conduct, which the church maintains is lived by tradition rather than by systematic rules. Rather than a packet of rules to memorize, the *Ordnung* is the 'understood' behavior by which the Amish are expected to live."[4]

Sometimes in a council meeting service a man is chosen to be an elder – either a bishop, preacher, or deacon, whichever is needed. Everyone who is a church member gets to vote which man they choose. The three men that are chosen the most are the candidates for becoming an elder.

One of the three men will also be chosen for the position by sheer luck of a book. They each have to pick up a German song book. One book will have the notice for the position inside it. The man who picks up that book is the chosen person.

Once the congregation knows who the chosen person is, they weep. It is as if they are in a funeral, weeping. The weeping is the religious belief that we must acknowledge the seriousness of the responsibility the chosen person faces.

The Amish have communion once a year. The elders take a large, round loaf of homemade Shepherds bread. They pull chunks of bread from it and pass it down each row of church members. Each person pulls a bite from it, eats it, and passes it to the next person.

---

[4] Donald Kraybill, "The Riddle of Amish Culture" on page 112.

After that the elders pass a stainless steel wine cup from person to person. Each person takes a takes a sip from it. No one seemed to mind drinking from the same cup that everyone else had drank from. When communion is over those who aren't church members leave the church service.

Now the church members get busy getting their feet washed by other church brethren. A bowl of warm water and a towel is passed as the women wash women's feet and the men wash men's feet. It was a sign of respect among the brethren.

I remember thinking to myself that I may disrespect God by not having communion after I leave the Amish. I didn't know that many non-Amish churches serve communion. After I left the Amish I figured out that non-Amish have communion much more regularly than once a year?

* * *

It was enjoyable preparation and hard work to get ready for church. I enjoyed watching my mother clean every wall and ceiling and every crack and cranny in each room while we helped. The floors were scrubbed by hand and everything was put away and stored.

With the cleaning done Mom now has to get new jars of fresh paint. Every can of paint has pretty colors, yellow, baby blue, soft green and peach. Every room in the house gets painted in fresh pretty colors.

With the painting done, Mom hangs new, sheer curtains in the kitchen and new towels in the bathroom. She bakes bread, mixes a peanut butter spread and sets out beets, pickles and jelly, etc. When the furniture is moved to the shed and the benches are set up in the house we are ready for church and a singing.

I looked forward to those times we had church in our home. We got to leave church early on those Sundays to fix lunch for everyone. My Mom and aunts helped each other prepare lunch while I played with my friends and cousins.

On Sundays when we had to sit through the service I would sit on a hard backless bench. My back ached which caused me to squirm continuously next to my mother. Mom would reach down and pinch my leg. How painful those pinches were! The elders tell everyone when to sit, kneel and stand which allowed me to change position momentarily and relieve the aching in my back.

* * *

I remember as a young child I would put pretty little flowered and lacy hankies into my pocket and play with them through the service. When I became older, I sat with all the other girls my age while watching babies play with their toys. They would play with many beaded strings and magnets and little toys that would not be considered safe and appropriate for 'today's' children, but this was the Amish world and we had our own rules.

My Amish friends and I would go to a lost and found bag that came to every church service, along with the bench wagon. We'd look through it to find abandoned toys and play with them.

In the middle of the service the lady of the house would pass a bowl of soft sugar cookies and saltine crackers. All of us little children would eat our cookies and crackers. After that I would see someone passing a water glass. I would reach for the water glass and then I wouldn't drink the water. The water had cookie crumbs floating all through it, after the other children had been drinking from it. Yuck, it looked nasty and I was so thirsty!

Dear Journal,

I had to sit for three hours in church today so I let my imagination wander. I wondered why we measured every little seam on our dress and why we were seen as evil when we didn't have everything sewn to the exact measures of Amish rules.

In our church the Bishop decided on exactly a dress length between the knee and calf, a waist exactly measuring one inch in width, a collar measuring exactly a quarter of an inch. The cape had to have three presses down the back, a long one in the middle and two short ones on each side. Our prayer caps were to be gathered, not pleated and have a crease exactly a quarter of an inch across the gathering.

Mind you! We are evil for not following the rules of the Bishop because Amish are next to Godliness. Everything we do is backed up by Bible scriptures and I find a scripture for everything.

I wondered why it's okay for Dad to be so angry but we are evil for not following all the Ordnung. The Ordnung is too miserable to understand. So, I imagine what it's like to be in another family, maybe Bill's family!

If I was in Bill's family we would all stand together like we were in a Christmas program and pull stunts between us. We would make everyone laugh and be the comedians of the year.

Edwin had a crush on me so he would pull stunts to get my attention. I pretended to ignore him but I really found it funny and I liked him.

We would sing the songs off-key and sometimes Levi would change the words to a bad word and we'd all pretend not to hear. Levi, He was spaced and clumsy and Darlene would reach out her foot and make him trip. Everyone laughed although it was really quite mean and Darlene said that she just couldn't resist when she noticed how spaced he was.

In my imagination we were not only funny but we dressed fancy and hid cell phones in our drawers so we wouldn't have to run to the neighbor constantly to make phone calls. We didn't have to can our food. It's such hard work.

One time Darlene wore pink panties to church and when we got there one of the elderly grannies picked her up and held her. She proudly told the granny she had pink panties and we were embarrassed. What if the granny disapproved? Mom said underwear didn't matter that much, just outerwear. Well, I know Amish people disapprove of pretty clothes.

I prefer a world of fantasy. In this fanciful world I was happy and I didn't have to hear the preacher yell about the terrors of hell. This was my day in church. Until I daydream again, at another church service.

Always, Regina

Our Amish Singings

THE AMISH DEFINITION of a "singing" is a place where Amish youth gather for entertainment and finding a mate for life to court and marry. "Singings" are a place where Amish youth eat a home cooked meal. It's prepared by the lady of the house who hosts the singing in her home. The youth sing High German songs for a pastime. Families in our community would take turns having church and a "singing" that same evening in their home.

In our community it is an adolescent custom and the *ordnung* for an Amish boy to get a girl to go on a date with him by getting a guy friend at a "singing" to ask the girl if she accepts the date. The friend will have to tell the boy whether the girl accepts the date or not. The boy will date the girl in her home if she accepts the date. The rest of the family will sleep in their bedrooms while the date is actualizing.

Yet I found Sunday afternoons far more entertaining than a date because my sisters and I would have friends over. This occurred between the hours at the end of church and before a singing began.

We'd take long walks in the country side, entertaining each other with conversation. We played songs on our harmonicas, played games together and popped popcorn in the old, fashioned popcorn kettle while gossiping about the 'wild' youth.

When it was time to go to the singing it required us to hitch a horse to the buggy and drive to the singing. We always hoped to have a boy take our horse to the barn and unhitch it for us, which they always did. When it was time to go home afterwards we waited for the boys to hitch our horse in the barn again and sometimes they did.

Sometimes we ourselves went to the barn to get the horse hoping not to see a boy taking a whiz. After Lamar got married we didn't have brothers to help us with transportation. We had to depend on others and mostly ourselves.

During our singings we would sit still and get very bored. We could also play games when we didn't have to sing, but no one implemented to play them as our older siblings used to. We forgot the fun they used to have.

Times changed before I became a teenager with fun replaced by serious adult thinking. After that fun became a faded past memory. The click-clack of square high heals my older sisters used to wear was replaced with wedge heals. The pretty soft blue and green dating dresses that snapped shut were discharged along with the innocence of touch. The old songs played on the harmonica were heard less and less. I watched an innocent time fade before my eyes, sometimes with a feeling of loss and sadness.

Above all else, I was relieved that we no longer *snitzed*, (a German word) Amish youth to welcome them to the group. I don't know how to tell what *snitching* means except that to us it meant an uncomfortable event was undertaken to welcome new youth to the singing.

I could still see the singing at Amos Yoder's house because the wild youth came to the singing that evening. The wild boys had their shirts open and their long hair hanging down their back as was the style then. The wild girls wore make-up, styled hair and baby blue button dresses.

Lenora's friends wanted to *snitz* her to welcome her in. They had a bag of applesauce, ketchup, pepper, horse manure and raisons and they were waiting for the singing to be over to shove it in her mouth and make her swallow it. It was a bullying, frightening experience, causing people to vomit helplessly.

Lenora was prepared and half way through the singing she got up as if heading toward the bathroom. She snatched the plastic baggy with the nasty crap from Lucy who held it and flushed it down the toilet.

Lenora declared the *snitzing* was ignorant and it became one of those things that became forgotten, a thing of the past. Now with the *snitzing* a past event we had a new grievance to deal with. It was our boredom at the singings.

An evening at a singing was dull while everyone sat looking at nothing in particular and said nothing of intelligence, nothing interesting. It was almost as if everyone was afraid to speak up and does something fun.

It wasn't all that bad for me because I had my friend Dora around to help me get through the boredom. I listened to her wacky stories and played her humorous games, realizing some of life could be fun. We watched all the prissy people and laughed at them, making jokes.

Dora didn't have a reputation to lose so it didn't matter. Her mother had left the Amish years ago, married an "outsider" and had two daughters, Dora and Miriam. She had an abusive relationship with her husband, and because of it she chose to divorce him. After this she returned to the Amish, forever doomed to never marry again after sinning so greatly.

She moved back to her parent's home while living in a small house next to theirs, cleaning houses for outsiders. This is where she raised her two daughters, while battling cancer for many years. She lived a life of much suffering.

I didn't have a lot of time with Dora because most of my time was spent working in Mom's bakery. I also spent much time at my sister-in-law Ann's house helping her after her anorexia possessed her, crippling her abilities to do things for herself. Little time was spent at a singing with all of my friends.

My friends were Katherine, Lizzie, Susan, Loretta, Sarah and Dora. Katherine was the pretty and the popular girl. She was flirty, giggling and vague. Lizzie was the plain one of the bunch and in fact her family was the plainest of the church. She wasn't prissy or stuffy and simply had a common air which made me like her. Susan was the Bishops daughter and she was neither popular nor outwardly plain. She didn't stand out but she was one of us. Loretta and Sarah were fun-loving and always fitting in. Dora, as we now know, never fit into the crowd.

Sometimes Dora was also too much for me as she lacked manners and became ruthless. When it became too bad I would momentarily leave her and spend more time with Katherine. Yet Katherine was not good at conversation, so I'd leave her after awhile and go back to Dora.

Dora and I had enough fun at the singings that we also planned fun events away from them. One such time we planned a camping trip. The camping trip was with my sisters Lenora, Teresa and Darlene. Dora and her older sister Miriam also came along. Not only was Dora my best friend but Miriam was Lenora's best friend.

We all had a blast on our camping trip. We made little mud pots with lids and decorated them. We splashed in the waterfall until Dora decided that skinny-dipping would be great fun. So Dora, Darlene and I jumped in the water naked until Miriam, Lenora and Teresa yelled at us.

The next day the camping trip was over and Darlene and I worked all day in the garden, picking tomatoes. While we were working Mom came to the garden, quite cross and told us we had to clean kitchen cupboards as punishment for skinny-dipping. Since Darlene and I worked in the garden most of the day Mom forgot about it.

The following day Darlene got a camera and started taking pictures of everything. She knew she wasn't supposed to but who was to know, except me? I wouldn't tell anyone. All of the wild youth had cameras and radios and no one took it from them. What would be different from Darlene?

I decided that if Darlene could have a camera, then I could cut my hair so I cut it shorter in the back. I also bought a white scarf even though I wasn't allowed to wear it.

My experience as a teenager in our community was that we had two types of singings. Both singings contradicted each other in style and behavior. One singing sang slow, somber and boring songs in High German and the other "singing" was a noisy, raging party with beer. It was impossible to have fun at the good singing and it was hard not to get involved in sex and drugs at the bad "singing."

Many communities don't split singings, but rather the good youth stay inside to sing and the bad youth go outside for a noisy disturbing party, which is how it used to be when my older siblings had "singings." Our community decided to split the singings, making us choose which group we wanted for ourselves.

The wild drunken singings were not prohibited by the *Ordnung* even though the Amish were aware of what was going on. After all most of the Amish youth were not church members and Amish youth can't be held accountable for any behavior defying the Amish if they aren't a church member. Whether the *Ordnung* was disrespected or a crime was committed, the Amish want to deal with their own problems. They had useless talks to the rebellious to change their behavior. The rebellious church members also made unrepentant confessions to the Bishop, believing their religion by its own merit made them good.

Therefore the "wild" youth in our community lived to disturb the peace of decent Amish people. They drove their cars past the home where church was held. The music would blast loudly from their stereos and everybody riding inside the car would yell insults at the church. They behaved likewise at a singing.

We also had problems with wild Amish teenagers destroying our properties and homes. We'd come home from church and find the house destroyed and things stolen. It was also not unusual on summer nights when my brothers, sisters and I would sleep on the trampoline to hear corn crackling in the garden. When the sun came up we would find a path of corn trampled flat in the garden and our large tanks of gas empty.

This is because many wild teenagers owned cars in our community. They would sneak through the garden and steal gas from our tanks to fill their cars with gas before Sunday night beer parties.

The intensity of how teenagers behave varies from church to church and state to state. I saw that each community is different and unique. One church in Ohio made all teenage girls dress in black to imply they are pregnant before marriage, which many were. In a community in Wisconsin, Amish girls are known for prostitution. One church in our state was known for requiring a dating couple to lie together in bed while they were on a date, but not in our community. In our community we had our share of teenage pregnancies and problems.

Easter was always a major party time for the Amish youth in our community. A three-day party of games and food was set for the 'decent' youth. A long and lengthy beer party prevailed for the wild crowd.

One Easter when the wild youth were having a beer party nearby we noticed that our dog, Fluffy was missing. We noticed the next day that Fluffy was still gone. We were ready to give up looking for Fluffy when he came home limping and drooping. He was a mess, looking hurt with the saddest look in his eyes. We all wondered what happened, knowing it was nothing good.

A friend – Lorene – stopped at our house later that day. Her daughter, Rebecca had been to the beer party, had seen everything that happened to Fluffy and told her mother. Lorene told us that two of the girls at the party had been very drunk. They picked up our dog and dropped him into the rocky creek bed below. Fluffy lay still without moving and they thought they killed him. Fluffy had revived and made it home, sad and wounded.

Whenever we saw those two girls after that they avoided us, thinking they had killed our dog. Despite all this we didn't call the police because we were Amish.

In fact, nobody in our community called the police and grounding Amish teenagers wasn't heard of. Corporal Punishment is used for little Amish children and not for Amish youth. If it would be used for an Amish youth it would come from a personal family choice, not associated with routine community parties.

The singings were a chaotic part of my life, along with hard work. Sometimes I sang to myself to bring humor to the situation.

I would sing, "Everybody hates me and nobody loves me, so I'll just eat worms."

"Big fat juicy ones"

"Thin long slimy ones"

Everybody just eat worms".

The Siblings in Our Family

MY MOTHER HAD ten children, from the oldest to the youngest, Mary, Jerry, Emma, Joe, Ray, Lenora, Lamar, Teresa, Darlene, and myself. I will not try to name nieces, nephews or other relatives because there were too many. My grandparents on my father's side had fifteen children and on my Mom's side they had thirteen. Most of my Uncles and Aunts have large families, as well as my brothers and sisters. As of today, I wouldn't know what more than half of them look like.

We had rare moments of fun together as a family. We worked hard and sometimes we enjoyed homemade ice cream dinners with our cousins. After the meal we would hang a white sheet over the double doorway to the kitchen and with the dim light of a kerosene lamp which cast shadows on the sheet, we played silent drama.

My brothers enjoyed pretending to be Santa Claus coming down the chimney. They also pretended to be surgeons pulling intestines out of patients. With a deathly ill patient lying on a table the surgeon would take a sharp knife and slice the belly of the sick patient. He would pull out a string of rags that looked like gut-wrenching intestines through the shadows of the sheets.

Our idea of having fun was staying up late and playing tricks on one another. One such trick was when Lamar opened the door and called for us girls to come outside. Teresa and Darlene ran outside and suddenly I heard them screaming. I knew something was up, so I went to the door and cautiously looked around. When I looked down at my feet, a rattlesnake lay coiled and ready to strike. I noticed the snake didn't move and realized it was a set-up because the snake was dead. It was a trick and a good laugh for Lamar. This made up most of our fun, but not all.

We had moments when we younger kids sang together while some of my older siblings played on their harmonicas, and others would yodel. In the summer my sisters and I gathered pebbles by the brook and made wishing wells. We also climbed the cherry tree, picked cherries, dipped them in a little bowl of sugar, and ate them.

My brothers, sisters and I spent hours picking grapes. They were very seedy which meant we had to swallow them without chewing. We often played together with the neighbor's kids, especially a boy named Peter. He was neither Amish nor from an Amish family, but we knew him well and grew up with him.

One day we decided to share our grapes with Peter. Biting into a grape, we could here him crunching seeds but he kept on eating grapes. He ate one after another crunching on countless seeds. We'd stare at Peter and ask, "Peter why do you chew your seeds"? He would shrug but than he'd want us to come to his house to watch television. We went to Peter's house to watch television and we talked among each other about Peter eating the seeds in his grapes, thinking it was funny.

I remember how we used to have fun with Jerry and his scary stories. At night we'd all sit outside on the trampoline and listen to him. He would take a flashlight and shine it around in the dark making it look spooky. We'd scream and laugh in anticipation as each story reached its climax.

We would sit in a group around each other, all ten of us children. We had our little fireflies stuck on our foreheads as Jerry starts the first story about a little girl and a liver.

The story began like this: *Once upon a time there was a little girl named Mary Ann who loved to eat liver. One day her mother discovered that she was out of liver so she sent Mary Ann to the store to buy some chicken liver. The walk to the store was very long so she dawdled and played along the way.*

Time passed and eventually night prevailed. Mary Ann still had not made it to the store and she realized her mother would be angry if she came home without the liver. In order to evade her mother's anger she needed a quick alternative.

Tired from her long journey, she stopped at a graveyard to take a rest. Suddenly she got an idea, a way to trick her mother. She could have a human liver and her mother would never know.

Mary Ann found a shovel lying next to a grave headstone. The grave belonged to a young child. She decided to dig the liver from the graveyard. She picked up the shovel and dug up the grave. Mary Ann cut out the dead child's liver and took it home to her mother. When she got home her mother asked her where she got the liver and she replied, "I got it at the store." Mary Ann went to bed that night but she couldn't sleep because her guilty conscience kept her awake.

At midnight Mary Ann heard creaking footsteps on the bottom stair. A voice said, "First step, why don't you tell your mother?" The second step creaked loudly and again a voice said, "Second step, why don't you tell your mother?" Mary Ann began to shake in fear. As she shook, she heard the creak of the third step and the same taunt, "Why don't you tell your mother?" The taunts continued until the tenth step was reached.

At this point, Jerry let out a loud, long scream, which scared us. This in turn caused us to scream and run away in terror while Jerry sat, laughing as he watched us run away. He would find us and tell us the next story. Now its bedtime and we are so frightened we can't go to sleep; therefore, we stay up late into the night.

Jerry was a fun-loving jokester and therefore we spent more time with him and had more enjoyment with him than with any other siblings. He would often play on his harmonica while we sat and listened to him. I would watch him hitch his horse to his buggy because I was fascinated by a small piece of adornment on the harness. It was an oval shaped green piece, with a picture of a horse head on it. I could still hear the clip-clop as he drove away while I listened to the faint sound of his harp.

Still, as a young man he learned to be cruel to animals. At times I didn't see his funny personality because I saw my father's behavior in him. As he became older and more like Dad, he also became more distant from all of us.

Jerry became uptight and harsh after his marriage, and his own children suffered in the gloom of his coldness. Darlene and I watched in concern as we became their maid. We missed his stories and his wife Louise missed his harmonica playing.

Growing up, Louise was also one of my better and more respectful teachers. Out of all my teachers she was the only one I didn't dread, didn't avoid. I missed her when she quit teaching school after the second grade because of her marriage to Jerry.

Times change when people grow up and time certainly changed Jerry. Between him and my oldest sister Mary, they were both growing up too fast. Or at least that is what mother said, and that is what made them grouchy.

Mary had a reason to be grouchy as she was responsible for all of us younger siblings. She worked too hard which made her very tired. She also had long, black hair that reached the floor and was quite pretty. She was talented and became a professional artist with a love for beauty. She painted beautiful pictures of scenery, detailing as uniquely as Tomas Kincaid.

I'd sit by her side watching her paint until she was annoyed with me. When she was upset with me for being in her way she'd pinch my ear. My fascination did not disappear because of her temper.

We all believed that Mary was the fancy sister because she loved pretty things. She wasn't the prettiest looking girl because at age sixteen she grew a thick, black mustache. Her appearance was less than receptive until she removed it.

When Mary was twenty-one, she took a long vacation in the West, met and married a man from Montana. She never lost her artistic touch but the pretty things she cared for faded away after she got married. She became old fashioned in her dress attire, *Ordnung*, and ideas.

As a young child she described my birth to me. "It was a dismal Halloween and nobody was expecting any fun, which disappointed everyone. Directly at midnight you were born and everyone became excited. Halloween became a happy day, after all."

Halloween was usually a happy day for us. My father and brothers would take the neighbors on hayrides and we always had a few masked visitors at our windows. They had hotdog and marshmallow roasts on the fire and it was enjoyable.

More happy times were when Emma stood in the doorway to the house calling, "Supper, supper." It was our indication to come to the house to eat together as a family. Later, as I got older we almost never ate together as a family. We became busy with Mom's bakery, always working.

Emma was a happy-go-lucky girl, so I stayed with her more often through church services. She was bright and cheerful, never seeming to worry as she lived with fancy-free fun. She'd splash all over the floor while she washed dishes, her little kerchief sitting crooked on her head. She had a kind heart and made the family fun and whole. She won our heart and became our favorite sister, succeeding Mary in her love for pretty things.

Emma married Bob who was part American Indian, red-haired and jolly. They had beautiful, dark little girls who showed strong Cherokee Indian characteristics. I took care of them many times always gazing into their pretty dark eyes and admiring their loveliness. Yet Emma was quite the opposite from Joe Jr.

Joe Jr. was a spitting image of my father. They looked exactly alike with blue eyes and a head full of curly black hair. Junior's hair color changed from blond to coal black when he was two years old. It was an unexplained change which nobody understood.

I don't remember Jr. talking or smiling much. He was quiet and unnoticed and I didn't know him well. He was like an absent brother, gone and forgotten. He was like a stranger passing and disappearing, as a shadow.

I watched him walk across the yard one day like a passing wordless ghost, his eyes expressionless. His silence worried me when I saw a bruise on his eyes. I didn't know how he got the bruise and in fact he never told me about it. Later that day my sisters told me.

It happened when he passed through the barn door trying to go home from a singing. It was the only door to pass through in that barn and two wild Amish boys stood in the doorway waiting to attack him. Junior waited for the longest time to pass through that door, but the boys wouldn't leave.

Mom and Dad waited at home wondering why it was getting so late and Joe wasn't home. When Joe knew that it was 3AM he went through the barn door knowing he'd be decked. He got paid the ultimate prize for being a decent youth with their punishment.

Junior married the bishop's daughter who had also been my bossy third grade teacher. She hid behind a silent, expressionless facade which erupted without warning. I remember their children could cause such a fuss and when you saw her face she looked calm and composed. Behind a closed door she could pound a hide like a bursting volcano.

Ray looked nothing like Junior, as he had blond hair and blue eyes, accented with thick glasses. He had many nose-bleeds characterized by a rough life. He was a good older brother always letting Darlene and I follow along as he did his chores. He taught us everything through showing and telling.

Ray was more violent with animals, even more so than my other brothers. It got to the point where it was terrifying to watch him. His temper often flared out of control, reminding me of Dad. Yet he was always good to Darlene and me.

He married a woman from a poor family named, Ann. She dressed stricter than everyone in the community, always wearing the longest, darkest dresses and the biggest head coverings.

Our family never had much of a relationship with Ann because she was socially backwards. She didn't know what sex was until after she married Ray, as her mother died before she spoke to her about it. So my mother spoke to her after her marriage with Ray.

Ray lived a life that was as poor and harsh after his marriage as Lamar's wasn't. My youngest brother Lamar was melancholy and gentle. Sometimes he spoke of difficulties since life was complicated for him. He often lagged behind his twin sister, Lenora, who was born first.

Lamar would walk to school with Teresa, Darlene, and me while we talked, discussing moments when we were scared or hurt. It was then that our silent life revealed its truth. Somewhere on an old, dirt road we were safe to spill our troubles. We were free to open up, to comfort one another.

Lamar married sweet, sensitive Susie. She had to be shocked when she met our family! We were loud and fought a lot and sometimes we were abusive. She was a gentle person and a good mother, very moral. She was raised in a comfortable home where she was provided good care, so unlike our own family.

Lenora was my magnet and had the spirit that Lamar lacked. She had a love for fashion, always looking for the prettiest, brightest Amish dresses. She loved to go shopping for nice things which caused arguments between Mom and her and also pushed the rules of the *Ordnung*.

Yet I needed her to keep my life from being dull. So we went shopping together at all the flea markets and planned adventures such as camp outs and building log cabins in the woods. They were little projects we started and never finished, but it was nevertheless adventurous.

In the moments we spent together, she would tell me stories like, "You made all kinds of weird faces when you were a baby and you squirmed constantly. You had blue eyes and curly, brown hair. Mom always made me rock you to sleep and the minute you'd fall asleep I'd call out to Mom to come get you. You'd wake up and start crying, so I'd have to rock you again when Mom entered the room."

Lenora married shy Marlin. Many years and eight children later, Marlin and Lenora finally decided to leave the Amish. They lived a life with Christian Mennonite beliefs rather than an Amish religion. It took a long time for them to change from Amish to non-Amish, but it was good after they changed. They became happier and so did their children.

I had another sister to build a good relationship with. I knew it was a positive step in the right direction. Lenora wanted to be a good mother and married a good man, living a good life. Like me, she was against many Amish teachings and against the abuse that occurred in the community, always declaring that abuse was cruel and evil.

Lenora was certainly more vivacious than Teresa, as Teresa was skinny and sickly with heart problems and weak spells. She stuttered seriously which irritated Mom and sometimes she talked in circles. Yet she related better to Mom than the rest of us, always nervous and flustered just like Mom.

Teresa was blond and blue-eyed. Growing up, she had a deep fascination with eastern medicine and new age magazines. She kept up with the latest natural health fads and had the skills of an artist. Artistically we were alike and sometimes very close in our relationship. We were each other's confidants, best friends and sisters. We shared art, poetry, and wisdom with each other.

Teresa also had moments when she was very dogmatic around me and Darlene. She would frighten us with her vivid description of hell and the after-life. Being Amish, she believed we would forever burn in a lake of fire. Furthermore she was my mother's one and only, home-birthed breastfed baby. Because, when Mom became pregnant with Teresa she wanted to try something new and different. So she planned for her first homebirth and breastfeeding while hoping for the best experience.

Dad ran to the neighbors to use their phone the night Mom started labor. He called the doctor to come and deliver the baby. He ran back home and waited on the doctor.

It was a blustery, windy, cold night when the town doctor came riding horse-back to deliver the baby. He was very drunk when he came in the house, swaying and slurring and mumbling under his breath. He immediately collapsed into the bed next to my mother in his drunken stupor.

Mother lay next to the doctor while in labor, smelling a sour smell of alcohol from him. He snored through a drunken sleep, not aware that he had a baby to deliver. So she wanted Dad to be with her but our brown and white Jersey cow went into labor the same time Mom did.

Dad then left Mom and went to the barn to deliver the calf. While Dad was in the barn for hours trying to save a calf Mom was laboring in pain, alone. In the end the calf was born dead despite Dad's attempts to save it.

In the meantime the doctor woke up long enough from his drunken stupor to deliver the baby. Mom thought the baby was dead when she was born, but the doctor dipped her into a bowl of water and revived her. My mother had accomplished her homebirth. She had a beautiful baby with a head-full of pretty blonde hair.

Yet in my mother's mind a calf was born dead on the expense of her own pain. The energy used to birth it could've been spent on her. My mother said the homebirth was a horrible experience, a nightmarish night never to be relived. She vowed never to have a homebirth again.

The rest of us were birthed in a hospital and bottle fed. Mom always spent two weeks in bed resting after a baby was born. In those days hospitals and bottles were normal with natural births and breastfeeding given no special recognition. "Amish babies in some settlements are born in hospitals, but many greet this world in birthing centers."[5] We didn't have education to support licensure in the medical field. We depended on the non-Amish world for counseling, doctors, and knowledge.

---

[5] Donald Kraybill, "The Quiet Spirit" on page 23.

I learned that when Mom was pregnant with me she was depressed. Everyone told me she changed her personality and became another person. I could understand that. She had a failure of a homebirth with Teresa followed by two miscarriages. When I came along the awe and excitement of having babies was gone after having many pregnancies.

Mom became pregnant with a baby boy six years after Darlene was born. The baby was a miscarriage and my mother never had children after that. She had been barefoot and pregnant for many years, carrying the tradition of the Amish until her life of bearing babies came to an end. Such is the life of my mother, and moreover of Amish women.

Miscarriages were common and frequent and rarely mentioned in our Amish community, thrown aside as unimportant. My mother never mentioned her own miscarriages and my sisters made little mention of it. Mom talked about her homebirth because it had brought her misery but she accepted her life as the "cross" she must bear.

Darlene and I had the closest relationship as we played and fought together. She was as aggressive and outspoken as I was reserved. She was the mathematics whiz and I was the artist and writer. Darlene and I both left the Amish and went to college but she became educated in business. I took care of patients in the healthcare industry. We each had one child; she had a baby boy, I had a baby girl.

My parents were as excited as any grandparents when Jerry and Louise were expecting their first baby. Darlene and I had much fun playing with the baby. We had more fun as more babies arrived and more siblings were married.

My older brothers and sisters had many babies, as my mother did. I loved taking care of their little children and I'd stay at there house to be their maid whenever they had a baby, which was often. I wanted to be the protector for all my nieces and nephews. Understanding that they had difficult times of abuse, I felt responsible to protect them. I needed to be everywhere keeping eyes on babies, but one day I realized I had too many children to watch. I had to let go of this responsibility.

Dear journal,

    The memories in my mind pull out the imagination. It makes me laugh. I remember the time I got Mom's little, green garlic capsules. I took them outside and squished them on the outside wall of the house. They were such a pretty green color when the sun shone through the old oak tree on the green juice. I imagined it was emerald juice and I could fashion it into the prettiest jewelry and were it around my neck.

    I always wanted a dollhouse, so what did I do? I helped Darlene build a doll house from the woodshed. Together we stacked up wood until we had a window, wall, and an opening for a door.

    We collected cardboard boxes and drew the makings of furniture. It was neat until my brothers carried wood to the house for the stove and the dollhouse was ruined. It was as close as we could get to a doll house and we sure had fun building it.

    One day we got one of the baby kittens and we put milk into this tiny bottle. The kitten chewed madly on the bottle and before we knew it, the nipple was gone. The kitten ate it. But she survived. How we laughed at the poor kitten.

    Our beloved pony, Peggy gave us all rides one morning. I had never had a pony ride before but Lenora guided him carefully, not bad. It could be fun, until Dad decided to sell Peggy and we all sadly watched her ride away.

    The funerals I attended as a child made a lasting impression. We were picked up by our parents and made to look in the coffin. Rather spooky! But we saw people from so many other ordnungs at the funeral and it was quite fascinating to watch.

    When I was a teenager I remember the Morgan David wine and the vodka we kept in the pantry. Once a year when we were getting ready for communion

Mom would put some in a cup, ask me to drink it and ask, "How did you like it?" It was okay.

I would sneak into the pantry and sip the vodka when I thought no one was looking. One day when I was going to the pantry I found Teresa sipping on the vodka and we laughed betwixt each other at our discovered secret.   Laughs and hugs, Regina

Ramblings of my Play and Friends

IN OUR AMISH community we were very familiar and informal around each other. We were not cordial and held to no mannerism. Etiquette and style were amiss. We never addressed anyone by, Sir, or Ma'am, but rather by their first name. We didn't address people as Mr. or Mrs. The ladies were named by their husbands name first and then their first name, for example John, Laura.

Our thank you and dining lacked formality unless we had a wedding or formal dinner. We weren't trying to hold to honor and style. We didn't hold to high society.

Amish men decide the rules of dress and certainly that is why much of it doesn't make any sense. We don't dress like the pioneers did and we don't even dress the way that Germans, Swiss, or Dutch dress. We don't just dress old fashioned. We take on a dress of many, many rules based on our religious beliefs. Behind it is the thought that it all comes from scripture.

More so we didn't believe in war or violence. It held no glory for us and therefore honor meant nothing to us, except to honor our religion. We didn't believe in self defense and used guns only for hunting. We weren't involved in education or politics. In fact, we were against it and perceived this as evil. We were Anti-violent, yes, except for those stories of my father's abuse and other Amish men as well.

We thought and perceived things differently from those who were not Amish. For example, our life and conversations were consumed about those who were plainer or fancier than us. We noticed little differences in the *Ordnung* and to us they were big differences. We made big judgments based on that.

In our daily life we argued, fought, laughed, joked and sinned as non-Amish people do. We rarely ate out or rather tended to preserve it for when we traveled. We ate store bought food and shopped from catalogs as any other people would. We had the same problems as the non-Amish world while lacking the same consequences and justice because of our restrictive religion. That is a complicated set up but it worked for us, however hard it is to understand.

Growing up in our community, I saw various positives and negatives of being Amish. A positive is that the Amish have a great economy. They hardly farm for a living anymore because they have a booming tourist business. More so, they hardly have any divorce and can usually support a large family. The church takes care of the poor, destitute people. They don't need to run to the welfare clinic or the food bank for assistance.

Our own family owned a large home, never suffered from poverty, and we were usually very productive. We had the finest china in America and beautiful furniture in our home. My mother ran a prosperous bakery from her home. Several other Amish women in our community also ran businesses from their home.

We had money for great investments despite my mother's fifth grade level of education. When my parents came to the middle age of sixty they had already retired into a brand new house close to my two oldest brothers and their families. They will be cared for in old age, by family.

Have you ever seen a homeless Amish person? I haven't. Yet I saw Amish people who did suffer from some poverty. In fact, the neighboring community next to ours held the yodeling Amish and they had poverty.

Indeed the yodeling Amish were so different from us that they fascinated us. They were the most old fashioned and the most traditional community in our state. Periodically we went to visit them to hear the yodeling. It was seen that they had no refrigerators and had food sitting in heat all day. We could give their children an ice cream cone and they wouldn't know what it was.

They had no running water but used a pail and dipper. Children would get the dipper from the dirty floor. They drank water from the pail and dropped the dipper back to the ground only to have the next child pulling it from the dirt for a drink. When the youth sat together to yodel, it was beautiful. However I was quite grateful not to live there.

Ann's family was the poorest family in our Amish community. They were seen as strange, uncaring and stingy. They always said that sick family members shouldn't go to the hospital because it cost too much money. People in our community talked about Ann's family, and other kids in the community made fun of her children. Ann appeared to be sexually abused, making allegations toward her father and brothers.

Ann had a history of deaths in her family. In fact her oldest brother, Harvey was hurt in a bad accident because he wouldn't use lights on his buggy while driving in the dark. He got hit by a car because the people in the car didn't see him and he also died in the fatal accident. His family wouldn't take him to the hospital, but fortunately a law passed that required all moving vehicles to have working headlights.

Ann's mother died from lung cancer when she was only sixteen years old and her grandma died later of old age. Her father married another woman she never liked and they had two children.

The oldest step-child fell from a bed, got a terrible bump and died shortly after his grandmother had rocked him to sleep one night. The second baby was a preemie who died two weeks after her birth in the home.

When the first baby died, everyone in our community declared that God killed the baby because they loved him too much and spoiled him. I was sure he died from the awful bump on his head and falling asleep so promptly afterwards.

Ann's first baby was stillborn. Mom went to visit Ann one day and Ann told her she hadn't felt the baby move in three days. Mom told her that this was abnormal and she should check up on the baby. Ann got checked and not only was her baby dead but it had been dead for so long that it was rotting inside her belly.

We had a graveside funeral for the baby with a closed casket. Years later Ann had another preemie and in a few months that baby died in the hospital. It was after she had her twin boys and she never had anymore children after that.

*   *   *

Looking at a more lighthearted side of events, our far-off Petershiem cousins from Mom's grandmother's side came to visit one day. Everyone spoke a serious Swiss-Dutch dialect and we couldn't understand them. Two charming little girls came along to visit as well. They were full of fun and in our eyes practically foreigners.

Mom cooked dinner for everyone and all of us little girls sat outside trying to get to know each other. The company tried to talk to us in their Swiss-Dutch dialect but it was too Swiss and it didn't make any sense so we switched to English dialect. As we talked we realized that they were from a small area where there was only one Amish church. Their *Ordnung* was quite different from ours.

We discussed the differences between our communities and talked about rules they had that we didn't have. We laughed and joked amongst each other while playing on our harmonicas and told stories we remembered about Jerry. When the company left we discussed the excitement of meeting someone Amish yet so different from our small Missouri community.

On another such day we had company from our far-off third cousins in Pennsylvania. We stared in amazement as they walked up to our house in what we perceived to be strange clothing. They wore black capes and blue dresses, whereas our dresses were always the same color – unless we wore an apron for housework. Little boys wore dresses. Why did their little boys wear dresses? We couldn't figure it out.

When dinner was over they pushed one another around and argued amongst themselves about who should wash dishes. Lettuce leaves and chunks of food floated in the dishwater when they were done washing dishes.

They wouldn't change the water, declaring it a waste. They said they couldn't have running water like we did and never wasted water. They scolded us for not scraping our plates clean. We stared at their strangeness in amazement, laughing and discussing it long after they left. Those moments of such company were few. After all, the relatives on Mom's side were long distance and tended to be more outlandish in our eyes.

Most of the relatives in Dad's side lived in our community and we would frequently visit our grandparents. I have many more enjoyable memories of those visits. Grandma would stand at the door smiling, greeting us. She had a little black doll in a doll carriage and a bunch of other dolls she bought at the store for us to play with. I would play dolls with my cousins while Mom would quilt with my aunts. Everybody brought in a dish of food and we had a potluck.

Lenora told me how I changed when I was a young child. "When you were a young child, we had gone to Grandma's house. Grandma said as she always said, "What a happy child she is. We'll never find a happier child."

"One day when we left Grandma's house you were a changed person and began to cry constantly. You kept clinging to Mom as if afraid. Mother didn't understand why you changed from a fast learning, happy child who became a clinger." Was I abused at grandma's house? I was so young I would never remember. We certainly had vulnerable moments when it could've easily happened.

In fact when Junior was two years old the neighbor hippy, a long-haired, free spirited man almost kidnapped him. He was playing in a fenced-in area behind the house because mother put him there to play. She wanted to make lots of room for running in a fenced area which would be safe for a two-year-old.

The hippy was driving past when he stopped the car and climbed out. He picked up little Joe and began to hold him. Fear ran through my mother's heart as a feeling that something was terribly wrong went through her mind. Mother ran outside, took junior from the hippy as she looked at him, asking, 'What we're you going to do?" The hippy never answered and after that he never acknowledged us, never waving to us anymore when he drove by.

* * *

On a late Saturday night Darlene and I sat on our bed chatting with each other. I sat in my little red Amish dress lined with purple buttons down my back. Darlene sat in a plain white full length cotton slip that my Mom had sewn for her. We discussed the day between us.

As we talked we shuddered at the thought of the dirty commode we had to drag across the snow drifts to dispose while we waited for a bathroom to be built. We marveled at the aspects of what our newly remodeled house would look like when it was built. We talked about how cute the baby kittens were in the hayloft.

We also discussed the terrifying scream we heard from the barn earlier that day. Mom had run from the house to the barn to check the scream and discovered it was our horse, old Nellie. She came back and told us that Ray had grabbed a pitchfork and rammed it viscously into poor old Nellie.

Nellie was our loyal family horse, our servant pulling our buggy to church. But at this time she was screaming in torture when she was forked like a steak, alive. Poor horse! I felt so sorry for her.

In fact, Darlene and I both felt sorry for her and we found the solace in the quiet of our bedroom where we discussed it all in detail. We asked one another how Father could be so cruel and how he could teach all the bad habits to our brothers, especially Ray. We wondered on our own fate discussing our own hardship, finding comfort in the bond of trust between us.

Our bedroom was the bedroom facing the living room with the big double doors. We had our little closet with "imagination Andrew" hiding inside to protect our baby dolls. Every doll was home-sewn with faces drawn on them. They wore little Amish dresses and aprons and were stuffed with cotton. They even wore little organdy caps for their head coverings and crocheted bibs and booties. We each had a diaper bag for our dolls. I had the brown handbag and Darlene had the red handbag. We kept strings of beads, rattles, bottles and flowered hankies in each bag for our babies.

Like all Saturday nights without a bathroom we had just taken a bath and the bath water sat in our room ready to get poured outside. Darlene and I were little and the tub was too heavy to pour.

Ironically, the bedroom door opened and Dad and Ray stepped in to get the bathtub. Darlene and I flinched as we remembered we had just been discussing Dad and Ray. They didn't seem to notice or perhaps didn't hear us. Then Dad stared at Darlene's long, white slip. Wordlessly he walked over to the bed, pulled up her slip, pulled down her panties, and struck her across the back. He picked up the tub, and he and Ray left.

Okay, he didn't like her slip, however large and plain it was and he punished her for wearing it. Funny, he never noticed it before today. Mom had often dressed Darlene in slips and usually Dad laughed it off like it was funny. Not today! At age three Darlene was never to wear her slip in the house because Father decided she was too old for that.

House of Our Memories

MY CHILDHOOD HOME was in a lonely house in the back hills of Missouri. It was close to a gravel road so isolated that whenever a vehicle passed we'd run to the window just to see it. A swing hung from an elm tree in front of the house with a square sandbox next to it. There was a rusty water pump sitting across the road next to an enormous field. We used commodes in the house and an outhouse outside, with an outdoor kettle nearby. My mother had two large gardens; including a cherry tree, grapevines, apple tree and a strawberry patch.

We had an old cave house in front of our house with washtubs hanging on the east side of it. A cave house is a small cellar built from a cave. The one we had in our yard was a small, rocky hill with a chimney sticking through the top of it. A small cellar built from a cave stood under that hill. Stone stairs rose from the cave (cellar) with stone walls on each side, making an entryway to the front door.

We used the washtubs for laundry and Saturday baths. We usually took our baths in the bedroom after carrying water in from the outdoor kettle. We had enough water to cover the bottom of the tub while Darlene and I shared our bath. When Darlene and I were preschoolers we'd take a bath in Dad's tool shop while Dad worked on his tools. That was so Dad could keep an eye on us and also because it was cooler there in the summer time.

Every Saturday, Emma and Mary (my two oldest sisters) put me on a green bar stool to braid my hair. My hair was braided so tightly I was sure it pulled my eyebrows up a notch, ruining my face. We all had our hair parted in the center because it was the *Ordnung*.

The clothes we wore were much more casual throughout the week than they were on Sundays. Women and girls had to choose whether they wanted to wear a bonnet and shawl. They didn't wear capes unless they had formal wear and then they wore the same color cape as their dress. We wore kerchiefs at home around the house and sometimes when we went shopping in town as well.

We hung our clothes on a line on laundry days. I didn't mind in the summer, but I minded in the winter when the weather was frigidly cold. The clothes would freeze solid before they were hung up. I remember feeling cross at my mother because she got to stay in the warm laundry room, while we were in the freezing cold hanging frozen clothes. Worse of all, at the end of the day, we had to go back outside and bring the frozen clothes into the laundry room to thaw out and dry.

I have toasty memories of heating our water in a reservoir on the stove while Mom kept crackers toasted on a shelf above the stove. Yet a tiresome chore that Darlene and I had was to churn butter in a big butter churn. We never used electricity and used kerosene lamps, stoves and refrigerators.

Yet things got more modern as I grew older. When my older brothers and sisters were dating and getting married, my parents had the house remodeled. I was five years old when they built a big bathroom and it was a relief not to use the outhouse anymore. My parents bought another stove and we used it to have hot running water in the house so we started taking baths more often.

They built two hallways, a pantry, a large laundry room and a basement, a bigger living room and kitchen, an upstairs and a porch. They took down the old swing by the elm tree and built a trellis with a large swing.

Mom built a bakery when I was fifteen years old and also fixed the compressed air. Now we could use it on our air fan and a few other appliances to give us more resources of modern conveniences. A few years later we had more gas equipment and started using car batteries and connectors to run various things.

When I was young the family dog was a spotted black and white fox terrier. We all enjoyed shaking hands with Spot and I cared a lot for him. When Spot got old and died we got another dog, named Shepherd. He was big and smelly with a heart of gold and he was very sensitive. He always looked so hurt whenever he heard thunder, as if it were a punishment. Later, we got an adorable white dog, named Fluffy. He became my favorite dog and he was very fond of me, crying often for me when I left home.

Our country home could've passed for a cat farm. We had many cats running around constantly. We had thirty cats one year, usually accumulating dramatically in numbers after we found all the litters of kittens. Darlene and I would find the kitties in the hay and tame the little babies.

We never wasted money on spaying and neutering cats. We didn't use a veterinarian unless it was a drastic emergency for a horse. Once a year Dad got his gun and killed a slew of cats. Mom would tell Darlene and me to hide during the cat shooting but curiosity killed our mind and we'd peek. The cats would fly into the air every time they were gunshot creating a nasty, disturbing sight.

When Darlene and I were little girls we had a great deal of fun using little kittens for dolls. We would put little doll clothes on the kittens and rock them to sleep. We lay them in little doll blankets and tried to keep them from running away. We put milk in little bottles with soft nipples and tried to feed the kittens.

One year when Lenora was mowing the grass she found two tiny baby bunnies. Mother bunny was nowhere to be found and Lenora didn't have the heart to leave the bunnies in the ditch so she brought them home. We fed them using a tiny bottle filled with milk. One bunny died the first night and the other bunny died in two weeks.

We had church in our house the last Sunday we had the bunny. We kept it inside the clothes closet so it wouldn't get trampled. It got minimal attention while we dealt with having church in our home, and the next morning it was dead. We didn't know what caused it but we were told it was difficult to keep any wild animal in captivity while keeping it healthy.

We had moments of simple joy in our surroundings, our home in the country. We would not have enjoyed certain moments more with modern assets. Likewise modern assets would not have created more unhappiness. In fact, it would be common sense to have modern assets, facing the inconsistency of our *ordnung*. Yet happiness is created from the mind. Somehow I knew that and knew I didn't have it.

I brought myself some peace while I sat on the large swing we had under the trellis with blue morning glories dripping through the trellis trim. Four o'clocks bloomed from behind me in the front row of the garden while wild flowers bloomed along the ditch.

I spent hours on the swing, drawing pictures of people while staring out into the horizon. I felt detached from the world past that horizon and felt a need to connect with something in which I was so separate. I drew pictures of Amish people and than I drew pictures of non-Amish people while dreaming about a day when I could leave while telling myself stories to keep my sanity.

The Amish Tyrants

*I*T WAS ANOTHER *hard day of work in the garden. I was working with my brother and sisters and we were all hoeing weeds and bagging potatoes. I wore a simple purple solid cotton dress, with short sleeves. I wore a brown apron tied around my waist and I kept filling my apron with potatoes, to store in the cellar. At times I stared at the blue sky drinking in its peace. At times I smiled at my own thoughts as I imagined times I wished existed, but I knew they didn't truly exist.*

My imagination snapped to reality when suddenly a raging, man with icy-cold, hate-filled blue eyes appeared in front of me, pointing a gun at my head. Looking into his eyes, I saw his rage and hate and it terrified me. Shock flashed through my mind and my whole body shook. I stared at the scene facing me. It was then that I realized the man was my father gunning me down in sheer revenge.

I looked around frantically and stared at my brothers and sisters. I helplessly pleaded and cried out for help. No one reached out to help me. They stared at me paralyzed by there own fear. Then they all turned their back and ignored me as if I weren't there. I was all alone, terrified, frantic, and helpless with no one to protect me.

I woke up from my nightmare . . . shuddering and feeling strange. Frightened!

I was twelve at this time as I climbed from my bed and pulled the curtain from the bedroom window and looked out. I took the time to soak in the beauty of the countryside. I looked through the fog and watched the sun come over the horizon while the mists rose from the pond. I looked through the fog in the pasture to see the horses. I could hear a freight train in the distance with the barking of our dog. The dog was running and barking as he brought the horses from the pasture. I realized the morning was beautiful and the countryside was mystical, enchanting.

I got dressed and ate a bowl of granola and then I headed to the tool shop to get the lawn mower and start it up to mow the yard.

As I was pushing the lawn mower and daydreaming as well, a disturbing noise distracted me. It was the sound of screaming from our pigs and I lost my daydream. Father was chasing them onto the truck and beating them violently, relentlessly. I couldn't help overhearing.

I knew that no one would make an effort to stop Father because it was a normal part of our life, a normal part of many Amish people's life. Father never appeared to assume guilt for the wrong he did to animals, and he even condoned the behavior as necessary. He'd remark, "It's the only way they learn."

I wanted Dad to see reason but I knew I couldn't argue with him. So I picked up my resolve and upon seeing Dad's little cherry tree, I clenched the lawn mower and mowed over the tree. I began to worry that I had overreacted and caused trouble. Nonetheless I finished mowing the grass.

I went into the house to eat at lunch, hoping for the best. We all stood around the kitchen eating our sandwiches and chatting. Dad casually leaned toward the window and looked out. I heard him asking, "What happened to the cherry tree?" I held my breath with tension building within me, expecting the worst. I heard Mom say, "Who cares, I never liked the tree anyway." What a relief, Mom saved the day! A smile went through me.

Later that day I gathered eggs from the henhouse. I gently shook the hen's nests, as always. I did this to stir the hens and make them rise. I could gather eggs from beneath them as they momentarily stood up.

When I vacated the henhouse father was standing in our driveway with a whip in his hand. A nervous, frightened horse tied to a post stood in front of him, ready to be whip-lashed. My heart hurt within me when I realized the horse had already endured a beating. I stood watching as Dad turned around and scornfully looked at me. He asked, "Don't you think it's cruel to shake a hen's nest"? But then his tone of voice turned mockingly as he asked, "Why are you looking at me?"

I was certain the chickens were unharmed. After all I didn't have the heart to hurt any living animal. Yet at the tone of Dad's voice, I tensed up and froze shortly as a feeling of pity and dislike went through me. Yes, I felt sorry for the poor beaten horse.

Suddenly my resolve built up and my heart began beating faster. I looked at him calmly, but feeling fear. I shakily replied, "Not half as cruel as you." Now I couldn't see the good in his religion anymore because what I had just seen and heard was typical bad Amish behavior.

As all children do, I made some mistakes when I was little, but Dad's rage was always inevitable. We all made our mistakes – such as those times when my siblings played naked in the hayloft until Dad found and whipped them.

Or the day my cousins came over to play for the day and I went home with them at the end of the day. I had found a chance to escape misery from the sadness of our home for a wonderful, short time. I spent the afternoon playing with my cousins and we laughed and talked for hours amongst ourselves, forgetting the time.

I heard a knock on the door and when I went to answer it my brothers, Lamar and Ray, were there. They laughed because I was wearing my dress inside out but they said, "We have to pick you up after we noticed you were missing." They had immediately assumed I was at the cousins' house. They said little to me on the way back and seemed lighthearted, bringing me back home with the pony and cart.

Dad was in a rage when I came back home. He came barreling across the yard with fire shooting from his eyes while terror gripped me. He grabbed the reins and gave me a beating of my life.

I made sure he didn't see me crying because I knew how much tears enraged him. Like a frightened child I ran, like the ground had fallen. As I ran, Aunt Lucy came from the outhouse holding cousin, Robert's hand. She asked me, "What's wrong, Regina?" I never answered but went inside the outhouse to hide from Dad's rage.

When I told Mary about the beating she told me about a time when she was a child. *"When I was a little girl I loved Grandma's little dishes. She had tiny pots and pans to make miniature cakes and she kept them all in the back of the buggy, the surrey.*

The back of the surrey had a small door and that's where I would climb in to see her cute little pans. I would taste her little cakes and admire all the different shapes of her pans.

One time when I went into the buggy as usual, I felt the buggy beginning to move. I was scared so I sat still until the ride was over. When Grandma stopped the buggy, she opened the little door in the back of the surrey and found me. She drove me back home.

I never meant to drive over to her home with her. I just happened to be in the buggy that day. Grandma didn't know it and drove me. When I got home I got the beating of a lifetime with the reins. "Oh Boy, was Dad mad!"

When I was grown I told him he was wrong for beating me for an accident and he replied, "I didn't know it was an accident, so it's not my fault. I believed him because he had no way of knowing." I thought to myself, he could've known if he had just asked. I wondered how she could be so ignorant.

Dad owned a lumbar mill when I was a young child. He would stand by his saw mill in his denim pants and suspenders, wearing a short sleeved button-up shirt with no pockets. He also wore a straw hat or a stocking cap while the boys worked the lumbar. He watched the boys work while I played by the oak tree nearby.

This was the family income while we were little children. It provided a comfortable income as the housing market in the Amish community grew along with the population. It gave me comfort to listen to the sound of the saw and watch the trucks load up the lumbar. Yet best of all I never had to see violence when he worked on the lumbar.

I saw violence when Dad was a pig keeper. He caused dread whenever the time came to load pigs onto trucks and take them to the market. He would load pigs on top of pigs already loaded on the truck, often causing pigs on the bottom to smother to death. We would frequently lose sales when the pigs came to market because dead pigs couldn't sell.

When Dad brought home the horses from the pasture, he shot them with BB guns and beat them once he had them in the barn. He also chased and beat the cow until she went dry from distress.

I remember one morning Dad had my brothers tie a halter on the cow and take her out for a walk so they could beat and jerk her around. Dad laughed at us if we showed him that we disapproved of his behavior. We went without milk that day because the cow was dry from distress. In my Dad's mind he was teaching these animals obedience, he was training them. After all he owned them for his own use.

It wasn't just the way Dad treated animals. It was the way many Amish men treated their animals. I didn't have to look far in our community to see the way that Amish men drove their horses unmercifully and beat them thoughtlessly, never considering it to be cruel. It bothered me tremendously and I pitied the horses in the disparaging life they lived.

Dad laughing coldly at my sympathy, saying, "Horses have no souls and no feelings." He also said, "Amish people are good because they don't have cars." It seemed to me that a car couldn't possibly be as evil as animal cruelty.

You also don't see car owners beating their source of transportation! It seems a good idea to respect that which services you, especially living, breathing animals.

One Amish man in particular stood out in my mind for his cruelty to animals. His name was Pete. He was the Bishop's son and shoed horses for a living. He kept an iron pipe in his shop to beat horses and also sexually defiled them. A simple church confession, however, excused him from bestiality so it wasn't worse than dressing against the *Ordnung*.

Horses would leave his shop limping and bleeding, half-crippled in torture. Yet some Amish men still took their horses there. We clearly didn't believe in using the humane society.

One day I found brother, Joe's horse in the pasture eating grass. The horse had one eye knocked out and I often wondered what happened to the horse to make her one-eyed. I continued asking others, "Why, is she one-eyed?" The answer was that Pete had beaten the horse in the face with his iron pipe. He had knocked the eye from the horse.

Pete was also a school teacher in an Amish school in our community. He beat all those little children until they were bruised and bleeding. As reinforcement for his bad behavior, brother, Jerry joined him in teaching school and joined him in abusing children. The behavior was accepted, or at the very least it was certainly not stopped by the bishop.

After church, we children got together and listened to stories about Pete's school. It was riddled with stories of children who had toilet accidents because they weren't allowed to use the toilet and were severely beaten when they had an accident. Many other similar stories followed, similar in nature to the previous stories but always a different incident.

Not only did I notice Pete, but I also noticed other things as well. For example, I noticed that men were above their wives with the wives submissive to them. In our community the women cooked and cleaned and had many babies while men over-saw everything.

Amish women were approved for being housewives although they didn't necessarily have to be one. Many women ran a business for the tourist trade. Yet we certainly didn't believe in fairness among the sexes and didn't practice it.

It was an accepted part of our life that marriages created a mate and a family, not romantic love. We scorned any terms of endearment. And accordingly it was certainly the men who made the rules.

This explains why rules are unfair for Old Order Amish women. This is true for any Amish community and not just our community. Women have to fasten their clothes with pins at all times, even during the week. Men can wear buttons all week and for half of their Sunday clothes. Women wear capes and aprons to be extra modest. Men don't wear any extra clothing. Men can wear any color shirt they choose. Women cannot wear pink, yellow or white dresses.

Furthermore, some men were known for bestiality. I knew Ray did bestiality as did few other men. I don't know why they did it but nonetheless they did it. Although I never saw such an obvious disgusting act I was horrified. It was unimaginable to know that Pete had sex with horses or Ray had sex with a goat. It seems it couldn't be accomplished unless some brutal act paralyzed the animals. Nonetheless I will not delve on how it was accomplished. These were admitted public church confessions and my thoughts are,

"How sick is that? It's completely revolting and gross!"

I was told that it followed uneducated people who knew little of sex. So I concluded that Amish men had sick desires and control issues.

I remember one day Emma needed to get woven carpets from Amish neighbors, an older couple. She took three-year old Cousin Victoria with her. Emma left Victoria sitting in the buggy while she went inside to get the woven carpets. The Amish neighbor man approached the buggy while Emma was inside the house. He violently penetrated Victoria, a cruel molestation. Victoria cried the entire way home and Emma could not figure out why Victoria cried so much.

I asked Victoria what was bothering her when she came back home. She wouldn't tell me what was wrong. I was worried about her but I didn't know what happened. She did not discuss this with me until she was twenty-one years of age.

I was also worried about little Darlene. She would often get a frozen, frightened look on her face whenever she had to go to the bathroom. Mom would angrily drag her to the bathroom until she had an accident then beat her in a fury. It was certain that something was wrong but she also wouldn't discuss it with me.

This was a difficult experience for Darlene, Victoria, and everyone else involved. Yet it didn't beat putting up with Dad. We managed to live through all the negative effects of sexual abuse. We learned to live with Mom's wrath. In the end, Dad was the most terrifying creature I knew.

We never knew when Dad would barge into the house. We (us children) flinched in guilt and fear when the screen door slammed on the porch. A chilling silence filled the air as we'd stare in terror while his cold, cynical eyes raked the room. He'd grab us and a series of beatings began.

Dad yanked off our skirt and removed our underwear. The beatings were long and endless. He didn't allow us to cry but it was impossible not to react. This enraged father more, but his eyes would turn to a cruel laugh if we showed pain. It was this sick, twisted pleasure that made me fear and mistrust him.

He beat us repeatedly without thought or question. Often the anger and beating provoked because we couldn't stop crying from receiving a beating. Usually we hadn't done anything wrong. We just happened to be too close to him at the wrong time and that was enough.

Dad liked to have devotions sometimes if the mood persisted. He'd make us kneel after breakfast and he would read the German Bible which we didn't understand. When he was done with devotions he'd pinch my ear. He'd wait until I walked past him and pinch, assuming I did something wrong but never talking about it.

Dad gave us beatings with the fly swatter handle before we'd go to church. He said it would make us behave in church. It was Amish discipline creating misery for us and through this I grew up tough, wearing an unbreakable exterior.

I may have been Amish but I wasn't sheltered. I knew a world of unjust behavior and knew how to climb my rocks alone. I worked double hard keeping the peace in the family and keeping my mother above the financial obstacles my father caused. I learned to acquire great results with great effort but it wore me out, keeping me broken and weary.

It appeared that there was a similarity between how Amish men dehumanized women, children and animals. My father beat his children like he beat his animals and women were confined to submissive and domestic duties. I believe the men saw it as there right. They didn't see it as a wrong. It was accepted and disliked by on-lookers like me. The outside world could not see the pain it caused. They couldn't even see that it existed.

Eight Years of School

EVERY FALL SCHOOL opened and basic education was given. A widely used school motto hung in our classroom as it does in most Amish classrooms, "Jesus first, you are last, others are in-between." As tradition persisted we quoted the "The Lord's prayer" every morning and memorized the golden rule early on in our school life. We didn't have any formal religious teachings and studied the main basics of education. We also had to learn some High German.

My parents had gone to public schools when they were little as did my oldest sister, Mary. When they were older they had an Amish school nearby and began to attend. My mother often commented on the better discipline and education in the public school.

In the Amish community, education did not play a big role. Both of my parents only had a fifth grade education and the rest of us only had an eighth grade education. We didn't have tutors or principals in school, neither preschool nor kindergarten, nor high school education nor a college degree. Also, Amish teachers in our community – or any Amish community – had no license or education to teach. We only needed enough education to succeed inside the Amish settlement.

In our community we worked as housekeepers, babysitters, farmers, and carpenters. We owned our own business if we were lucky. We owned stores, bakeries, restaurants, buggy shops, etc.

Corporal punishment was required in our school but Amish parents could decide independently on the level of discipline at home. And most Amish parents did indeed choose corporal punishment.

The school I had as an Amish student was as primitive as the plainest Amish could be. We had an outhouse for toileting needs and a water pump for water. It was plainer than the set-up in our Amish homes. I saw other schools with restrooms and running water, but not our school.

My friends and I would peek through a big hole in the boys' wing which was built to their toilet. We would watch the boys with their pants down, laughing at our mischief. We were not any less curious because we were Amish, and we were more degraded in our restroom privileges.

The worst thing was the girls' toilet. The door did not lock so I never knew when somebody would barge in, unannounced. I had a hard time using the toilet because I always felt tense and nervous. Worse yet, we had a three seated toilet and we all sat side by side as taunts and dirty talk was exchanged. We had no respect or dignity, nor did we expect it.

Everyday I would stay late after school to finish my schoolwork. My teacher did not believe in homework so I had to finish everything in class or stay after school to finish it. I had chores to do at home as most Amish students did.

The first two years in school were not as bad as the rest of the years. I had a nice teacher whom I liked better than my other teachers. She was rather fun and school life was a little more normal. Her name was Louise and when she quit teaching she was the first in-law to become part of our family.

All my other teachers were dreadfully harsh and thus I learned to dislike school as most students do. This started when I reached the third grade and I had a different teacher, named Leona. She was the bishop's daughter and she was also creative, very bossy and strangely silent.

That year my math grades started falling and she requested that I practice math during my entire summer vacation with Emma. I did this until I became sick and tired of it. Leona married Joe Jr. after she quit teaching school and became the second sister-in-law to join our family.

My Aunt Lynette was an older unmarried woman, called "old maid" (Amish people called all single women "old maid"). Lynette taught school for several years, always used bad grammar, like "ain't" and "cain't." She was a nervous wreck and constantly snapped her fingers, and her hair went gray when she was only sixteen years old. It was odd, but she simply woke up one morning with gray hair. The reasons were unknown, but it figures why she never got married.

Brother Ray taught school for a few years. I didn't have many friends before he taught school, and I had even fewer after he began teaching. If it were possible for school to get any worse, it did. A cold animosity set in now with the whole school hating him and now also us younger siblings. I learned to live each day in dread.

Pleasure of play and childhood did not exist for me at this school. It was more so for me than others, as I felt secluded with unpopular relatives teaching school. It was also because I didn't fit into their year-round baseball game, which was played also on snowy days. It was the number one sport in our school and it's yet another example of how I felt different from those in our community.

I was terrible at baseball and everyone who played baseball made fun of me. Now I had a choice between playing baseball and standing in the corner by myself. I was lonely when I didn't play and miserable when I played. I enjoyed volleyball and kickball and was relieved when we played other games such as running and thinking games, which were rare.

That was hard enough in itself but it didn't stop me from having an enemy during my school years, a girl named Edna. I thought she was a spoiled child, reminding me of Nellie Olsen from *Little House on the Prairie*. She'd make life miserable for me, but I couldn't avoid her and she wouldn't leave me alone. She picked on me and I thoroughly disliked her, creating more conflict in school.

To top everything off, I still had to deal with Dad's temper at home. One morning at the age of eleven I complained to Dad about my dress, which was outgrown and uncomfortably tight. He lost his temper with me and began to yell in a threatening manner. I ran to the back bedroom and locked it so Dad couldn't hurt me. Dad threatened to kick the door down if I wouldn't open it, so I opened it. He made a fist and pounded my back. My sisters scolded me for opening the door, and at once I wished I hadn't been so obedient.

These troubles stole my focus, and as I struggled my teachers belittled me for it. Now my parents, teachers and enemies became a problem that consumed my worry. It caused me to be a people pleasing person, playing a doormat role. Mental games were the teachers' role and mockery the students' role. This form of chaos was created through all our dysfunctional behavior, affecting my mentality and academics.

I wanted to disappear altogether from a world where I suffered the grief of conflict. So one afternoon on the way home from school I stopped in my tracks. I stared at the place I called home, and it seemed too miserable to go there. I faced away from the house while thinking about running away but I stopped, hesitating. I didn't have any necessities with me and running away was thoughtless without things I needed. I slowly walked home with dread.

Mom sent me upstairs to fix one of the beds when I got home. I walked up the stairs to fix the bed but my heart was not in it because I was dreading school the next day. I was feeling my pain and it was so deep that it hurt physically. I wanted to die, to end my misery.

I stopped making the bed when I was half done. I started thinking that life was not worth it, living in desolate existence and thinking about escape. Death seemed like a good escape, after all. So I started going downstairs to get Dad's gun hanging on the basement door. It seemed easy to go to the basement and shoot, ending everything.

I was half-way down the stairs when my thinking cap came to gear. I wondered if God and hell actually existed. After all, that was all I ever heard about in church. I finally turned around and went back upstairs, deciding not to kill myself.

I thought that God and hell might actually exist. I didn't want to be tortured with a severe burning in an eternal hell after being taught that suicide was an unforgivable act. Why should I die while my misery continued, creating a lost cause?

I didn't tell anyone how I felt, knowing they didn't understand or care. I knew I didn't understand death and the after-life either and so I wouldn't risk it. It was a disheartening life, but I learned to attain a mental attitude of determination and perseverance.

The eighth grade was the worst year of all. School was already chaotic and now it was a mad, out-of-control circus. We had three teachers that year.

The first teacher, named Amos, was an old man with a severe hearing loss. He had no teaching abilities and school became out of control in one week. He punished students when they did nothing wrong and never caught them in the worst acts of mischief. Every student took advantage of him, using him and making him the mockery of the entire school.

While he taught, I didn't learn anything in school. I'd start my mornings by asking cousin, Dorothy for the math answer sheet, and then I'd copy my answers. Recess was also a time for us students to sneak inside the classroom and copy the answers to our assignments. After copying our answers it was time to plan mischief for class-time, and we had plenty of ideas.

Once seated in class the entertainment began. We students sat and threw pencils at the students in front of us. Than we exchanged seats and told each other story's, leaving the classroom at free-will. We littered the floor with pencils and papers and crumbled papers loudly. We exchanged notes to one another while laughing at the antics of our class, enjoying the constant uproar. It was certainly better than the grim reaping of Ray's teaching.

One day, when Levi did nothing wrong, Amos made him stick his nose into a circle on the chalkboard and sat behind him with a paddle. We sat there watching him in disgust, thinking he was stupid.

I remember when I was in second grade and Louise taught school we'd think spankings were funny. Now we thought it was cruel and disgusting. How times changed!

Two weeks passed and one morning our teacher announced he would be fired. We didn't care and we were merely humored by his announcement. We had managed to defeat the worst teacher in our quest for fun. We learned to disrespect discipline, which was poorly administered.

The next teacher we had for that term was much better. We had a lady teacher with a gentle nature but this teacher had no intention of staying. It was a temporary fix while we waited for a new teacher to be hired. She usually had the respect of the students while she was teaching school. This was because we had to respect her because she was the parent of the most popular students in the entire school.

Brother Jerry was the last teacher we had for that term. Every student was subject to his cruel beatings, receiving bruises, welts and bloody marks. Jerry punished all us students for being "out of control."

He made sure we feared and obeyed him but he couldn't make us like him.

We all hated Jerry and there were many complaints, but nobody tried to stop him. Some parents who didn't abuse their children got angry when students came home bruised and bleeding, while other parents didn't care. The Amish bishop in our community didn't allow anyone to stop abuse. He would shun people for reporting it.

After the loss of popularity with so many of my brothers teaching school, I was completely surprised when two previous friends started being kind to me. One of the girls was cousin, Dorothy and the other girl my friend, Eliza. They wanted to have a sleepover at my house.

I wondered what possessed these girls to be interested in a sleepover, but they were not in the sleepover long before I discovered what they wanted. I was fifteen years old, subjecting my body to sexual activity so my friends would like me. It was a long miserable night.

All of the older students in school smoked, so Darlene and I learned how to make funny homemade cigarettes that year. My first experience learning to smoke was at Uncle Jonas's house. I coughed through my entire cigarette smoke while my cousins laughed. As time passed, I smoked more often when I was alone and worried.

Amish people in our community did not approve of smoking, yet at the same time they didn't make any attempt to stop us. Many of us smoked, and it became more common as the years passed. Dad never beat me for smoking. In fact he never found out.

I didn't want to finish the eighth grade. It was just too utterly miserable. My parents didn't care if I dropped out of school. Mom would use me to help her work at home. I didn't care to help Mom, but it was better than school.

The school board disapproved of me dropping out of school. I finished the eighth grade and was relieved when that was over. Behind me lay the memories of harsh teachers and mocking students.

Dear Journal

    The neighbor kids, I and my siblings would all walk to school together. Our walk would never end because it was endless. It was like the little spice holder we had in our cupboard.
    I would stare into it for hours. After staring for a long time I could see many stories of a house. The first story was full of furniture and the second story full of light. The third story full of church rooms and it never ended in its flight. Finally I could see a glimpse of six stories in one little spice holder, full of holes and slots. I could see more if I wanted to, endless!
    This was our walk. It was an endless winding road of trees, forests and pastures. We saw wild animals, singing birds and a conversation that never knew the word goodbye. In this world we were happy, forever. I was Alice in wonderland where nothing made sense and none of it mattered.
    We laughed at the running deer and gathered flowers in the pastures. We watched every shape of the clouds and bounced along them. I saw myself pushing a baby carriage along the little blue road. It had the prettiest baby inside and I was the mother.
    If I stared long enough I could see a rainbow move inside a living room and hide under our couch. I could hear the treadle of the old sewing machine. I could see the sun shine into the rainbow and duplicate it. It was beautiful, so beautiful!
    I imagine how it would feel to wear a white dress, perhaps with a lacy slip. Maybe we could have Carriages instead of buggies and we could trim the carriages in different colors. We could sit on the carriages and wear pink dresses with ruffles. That would be darling!

                                    AS Always, Regina

My Sentiments and Distress

MY OLDER BROTHERS and sisters went to an Amish school that stood in the middle of a Missouri prairie. I never saw the school much, and it got torn down just before I would've attended it. It was called the Prairie school and stood isolated and small with a reputation.

Mary was the teacher at the Prairie school. She was only sixteen years old, young and inexperienced. She was disrespectful to the students and in turn disliked by them. This attitude portrayed well and caused much corruption.

Due to Prairie School's corruption my brothers and sisters told me many stories about it. In all their stories I learned the sheer harshness of this school and the tears it caused.

It caused non greater tears than the one my youngest brother Lamar suffered. His gentle, meek spirit made him vulnerable in a harsh situation. In the wake of his sensitivity, he suffered a public ridicule.

Mary had Lamar fail a grade publicly in front of the school. She belittled him in front of the whole school while she did it. She berated him so badly that he ran crying from the classroom. After Lamar left the classroom, Mary sent Ray outside to bring Lamar back inside. Ray brought Lamar back to Mary and she belittled and berated him again in front of the school.

That evening Mary complained to Dad about Lamar's school grades. Dad gave Lamar a beating, declaring that low school grades deserved a severe punishment. Lamar had many emotional problems after this and became suicidal. He told Lenora that the only thing that kept him from committing suicide was his fear of death.

Lamar would get Dad's gun whenever he was suicidal. He would go outside with the gun during the night, contemplating suicide in his mind. Something always stopped him from killing himself, whether he had an interceptive thought or an unexpected distraction.

I began to realize that Dad's gun reminded me of a lure toward suicide. It was my gun when I wanted to escape misery and Lamar's gun when he felt hurt. It was Dad's gun when he was in a rage and chasing cats and horses. It hung conveniently on the basement door.

Not only that, but each outhouse in each Amish school portrayed a story that could make a person shudder or laugh. Myself, I found them shuddering rather than funny. Uncomfortable, no doubt! They were very uncomfortable.

Once more in this school the outhouse was rundown and broken. The lower back wall of the girls' outhouse was torn off. This left no privacy or dignity for the girls to use the toilet so the boys would run behind the toilet to watch the girls pee.

Mary would see the boys behind the toilet looking at girl's bottoms. She would yell at the boys to make them leave, but when she left they resumed there mischief. The girls got tired of it but they couldn't stop the boys.

Lenora was using the toilet one day when a neighbor boy stuck his hand under the toilet hole. She peed on his hand and he quickly removed his hand. Everyone howled with laughter, but this did not stop the peeking boys. They became more cautious where their hands went. Nonetheless this story lasted for years and the girls believed the boy got what he deserved.

The seventh and eighth grade girls and boys would all go to the outhouse together and tell each other dirty stories. It was their way of having fun. In those days it did not cause outrage by anyone because the "times" were more primitive and perhaps more innocent than today. It is not known if it was particularly noticed and if so, not with alarm.

I found all these facts troubling and found ways to escape reality, ways that others in our family couldn't understand. I had to save my mind and chose to save it by escaping the world, if only for a moment. I frequently went to the attic to read books and magazines by the stack. I had a tall imagination, learning quickly that the imagined world was far more pleasant than reality.

I would make my homemade cigarettes while I sat in the attic. When I was done rolling my smokes, I'd put them in a red heart shaped box. I would pull the insulation from the walls and hide my smokes in the wall behind the insulation. I didn't want my mother to know that I smoked, knowing she'd disapprove.

My books brought me joy and the knowledge inspired me. I puffed on my cigarettes and dwelled thoughtfully on each story, deciphering what I believed and determining which path I should choose.

This became my daily life where the only noise I heard was the drama of another story until Mom called up the stairs, "Regina, get to work and make yourself useful; reading isn't useful."

Mom made it clear that all my reading and daydreaming irritated her. Sometimes I forgot myself and daydreamed aloud until Mom's yelling and nagging brought me back to reality. I would think, "Crap, not again, I am happier in my daydream."

Mom would nap frequently throughout the day and night. She'd wake up and the bedroom door opened with a loud click while she'd emerge from the bedroom fretting and worrying loudly. She constantly nagged us and especially nagged Dad for not working and helping her.

Her daily theme was, "Dad, I need help, when can I expect your help, I'd like to know?" His correspondence half asleep on the recliner, was always, "Let the girls do it, the kids can do the work." Usually we were already busy working and Mom couldn't pull us away from current duties.

Dad wouldn't make any effort to move from his position on the recliner and Mom got frustrated. Sometimes she hit him with a flyswatter if he ignored her nagging too long. I turned a deaf ear on my mother and shut out as much nagging as I could.

I confronted Dad myself one day. "Do you think it's fair to sit while everyone else works?" He stared at me for a long time and said nothing. Darlene would push his buttons aggressively, to set him straight and tell him forcefully that he was lazy. But me, I wouldn't do that. Oh no, not me! I knew to choose the right moment and run.

My sisters realized that Dad really didn't like to work and Mom was overworked. Dad sat snoozing all day while Mom made business plans. While this evolved my sisters would tell Mom, "Don't start a business, Dad will come around." Dad never came around and in fact created more debt. My mother was a weary waiter and opened her successful bakery business.

I began to believe that my mother was a slave to herself. She worked unearthly hard providing for all ten children while tolerating Dad's laziness. She didn't believe in divorce so she quieted us children with food so we wouldn't do anything to stimulate Dad's wrath. In the end she took it upon herself to take care of everything.

She made Dad promise not to be cruel to animals before they married, understanding his raging anger. She knew divorce was not an Amish option. Dad promised Mom he wouldn't be cruel but broke this promise just two weeks after the marriage. It took two weeks to create a miserable marriage and it lasted an entire childhood for us children.

I grew up wishing my parents never married. A day didn't pass that they didn't argue and fight and a meal didn't pass without arguing. It was constant and ongoing without relief. I was certain that many of our daily problems were created from the tolerance of a long and miserable marriage, not to mention our religion.

Darlene and I had eating problems while we were little girls. We had a habit of gorging and purging. I would vomit several times before I'd stop eating. I wasn't overweight then.

I quit throwing up as I became older but still ate too much. I became an obese teenager who was desperate to lose weight. I went through hours of exercising, using large amounts of diet pills and laxatives. I also practiced being a vegetarian during this time to lose weight. My father never praised me but he would brag to others on my devoted health mindedness. Myself, I think I was simply trying to deal with stress and had the health effects of it.

My father's rage possessed me to play a game with him, a game of survival and luck. In this game he was Tom chasing me down and I was Jerry always escaping. I hid in my hole, quiet and alone, never crawling from my hole.

In other words I was always protected and sheltered in the outline of the crowd, never daring to venture too far because I knew my family wasn't there to protect me. I had to fight for my own needs and wants, losing what I couldn't gain and gaining what I acquired.

I felt as if I was in a terrible, terrifying trap where religion was more important than a terrified child's safety. I had no police, social worker, friend, or hope. We lived in a religion where the bishop shunned people who reported abuse. Therefore I felt cornered into a hopeless trap. Unless I left the Amish I wouldn't see what justice looked like.

Years of Turbulence

SOME PEOPLE MAY honestly enjoy being Amish. Others may hate it and fear leaving it. Many, I presume bear it as "the cross they must bear," a religious necessity. They believe they must honor their mother and father and stay Amish. Certainly I believed in honoring my mother and father, but I needed to come to terms with respecting them with the differences of belief and opinion between us.

I certainly didn't have the right personality to be Amish. My practical, common sense 'way of thinking' contradicted the common sense that the *Ordnung* lacked. I was a dreamer and an artist and I could never truly embrace myself in the Amish world.

There were wonderful moments and things that could be missed if one left the Amish. For example one summer we got a piano harp and I would sit outside in the starlit night and play. Old Rex, the dog lay at my feet, howling at the songs while coyotes howled in the distance. It was mystical and beautiful. Certainly it held an old charm.

It was as Lenora would say, "I want to leave the Amish but I may miss some things, such as the freight train whistling in the distance. I may miss the fog rising early in the pasture or the whinny of the horses." I might miss the baby kittens coming to me as I hang washed clothes on a clothesline, smelling fresh downy softener. I may miss the call of the rooster early in the morning and watching the bees buzzing around the flowers. Again, it's like I told Lenora, "It's the beauty of the country, not the beauty of the religion." She agreed. We lived in beautiful country and a nice big house.

We had good seasons, like in the fall during hunting season when my sister-in-law Louise would bring the babies to the house and we had fun playing with them as she visited with Mom. The men would leave us in peace while they stayed out on their hunting sprees.

One of our hunting seasons became more interesting when a friend of Lamar's, an Indian, went hunting with him. The Indian had long, black flowing hair and sharp, yet inexpressive eyes. His name was Running Bear. It was strange to see an Amish boy and an Indian being friends, but it was very nice

I was fascinated with Running Bear as I watched him glide across the room when he walked, as if he were an approaching shadow. He was beautiful and uniquely different from us, breaking the monotony of our life.

Our family had pancake brunches every day that fall when Running Bear was there. We eagerly waited every day for the men to return from hunting, listening to their stories and capturing each interesting detail. When Running Bear left us and walked all the way back to South Dakota, I missed him and his stories.

After Running Bear left, I began to spend more time thinking deeply about our Amish religion. I desperately wanted to leave the Amish, but I didn't want to pay with an eternity in hell by an angry God. I wanted to believe it would bless me but I had no way of truly knowing.

A dream came to me, one night. *I was lying out in the meadow feeling peaceful, knowing I was going to die. I was lying there when suddenly a terrible feeling of guilt overpowered me. The intensity of guilt urged me to frantically pray for forgiveness. I prayed obsessively but regardless of my constant praying, I felt worse. I didn't know if I had done anything wrong but I felt a need to keep on praying. I was afraid of going to hell and I wanted to make sure I was right with God, yet I couldn't prove that. I watched the sky pass overhead looking for signs of the end of the world, but I saw no signs. I struggled with my frightened heart, the unknown, a terrible fear of dying. Finally I began to have a sense of peace.*

Yet I woke up sweating and tense, distrustful. I contemplated my dream. I knew I had a terrible fear of God as a young Amish girl, after hearing many horror stories about hell. The Amish taught me that God might approve of me if I dressed plain enough. He might extend favor to me if I followed the Amish rules. I might have hope of getting to heaven, but only if I tried hard enough. And yet, it seemed hopeless.

Moreover, I was taught that mocking God was unforgivable. If I accidentally said the wrong thing and committed the unforgivable I was doomed to hell. We were barely given a chance to express any defiance against our religion without it being called mockery. That made me feel that everything I did was an open book for judgment and possibly wrong. I wanted heaven but I feared that I would do my very best and God would still find a fault, damning me to hell.

This fear consumed me so I began to pray fervently for forgiveness. I would ask God to forgive me and five minutes later, I'd ask God to forgive me again. Yet it never made me feel better or proved anything about God's judgment.

We were taught that it's pride to believe that we're saved. "The Amish are reluctant to say they're sure of salvation. The faithful, in the Amish view, are called to yield to God's will." Furthermore, the Amish believe that living in the Amish *Ordnung* and *Gelassenheit* is the will of God, "and rest in hope that things will turn out for the best."[6] It seemed to me that one need not bother with that hopeless hope.

My thoughts about the unknown made me miserable and proved nothing. I wished to not be tormented by them anymore. I realized one thing; the thoughts were unwelcome and came uninvited. The more I worried about them, the more they persisted.

I kept telling myself many times that I didn't believe my thoughts, rejected them and paid no attention to them. Every time I told myself I didn't believe my thoughts, the less I thought them. I began to preoccupy myself more with thoughts of rejecting my unwanted beliefs and I did this persistently. I replaced those negative thoughts with good ones.

One day at fifteen years of age as I was reading a book I realized that the thoughts no longer resurfaced. It was as if I had forgotten their importance. I knew then how important it is to learn how to use

---

[6] Donald Kraybill, "The Riddle of Amish Culture." Page 36

the mind more effectively. I realized the power I had within myself to change my own thought process.

My mother could call me "stupid" all she wanted, and often she did, but in the end she only had a fifth grade education and I had trained myself how to rethink my life.

A Secret Breakdown

I DIDN'T DATE during my teenage life. I never got asked on a date and I really didn't care. It didn't bother me because I was not attracted to Amish boys, and I found them rather disgusting. I don't know why Amish boys didn't look at me then. I don't know why so many guys look at me today. Perhaps I look better in non-Amish styles or if that it is just the way it was always meant to be, but it's alright. Either way, I have no regrets about it.

Dad would sit at the table and suggest that we, his daughters, should go out on a date with a boy named Carl. Carl was an Amish boy with a bad reputation for raping girls, and we had a dislike for him and mistrusted Dad even more for suggesting this.

Dad clearly didn't have his head on straight when it came to relationships. He couldn't possibly have mentioned a worse idea than dating Carl and furthermore he didn't know how to respect his own marriage.

In fact, one day Dad came home from town business. He was in the midst of an egotistical moment after meeting a woman in town, and he was telling us about her. She was the cutest woman on earth, according to my father. Her perfume smelled wonderful and he was sure she found him attractive.

Dad met another woman shortly after this incident. She was beautiful according to him. She had peaches for cheeks. Her smile was wonderful and he adored her charms. He was sure she found him attractive because she smiled so prettily.

Then Dad met the foot doctor and began to spend more time with her. The foot doctor was a single Amish woman, named Ellen. She had a reputation with men, and it wasn't an innocent one. She was a sexual friend to Uncle Harley, and in a small Amish community rumors abounded. It made it even more scandalous that Harley was already married to my Aunt Leah.

Mom would tell me she didn't trust Dad after spending so much time with Ellen. One time when Dad came home late after being with Ellen, I heard Mom yelling, "What are you doing, smooching around on other women?" Of course, Dad denied that.

Dad behaved like a cheating spouse, although we had no proof he really did this. He bothered and annoyed Mom greatly and worried her unnecessarily. We listened to Dad's stories although they were stupid and inwardly disgusted me. We turned our head from the problem and hoped Dad would just shut up. He didn't shut up, nor did my parents stop arguing about practically everything.

Perhaps my parents conflicting relationship had nothing to with Darlene and my relationship. Yet it did seem similar because as my parents fought, so did Darlene and I. We had many squabbles when we were teenagers and simply didn't get along with each other. We were complete opposites with personality conflicts creating our differences.

One time Darlene and I were having one of our usual arguments. It was a rather simple argument about a dress I had thrown into the corner of the closet. Darlene wanted me to hang up the dress. I refused to take orders from my younger sister. Besides, I didn't care about a dress lying in the corner of the closet. It didn't seem like a big deal, but it was to her.

Lamar was in the room next to ours. He was listening to us arguing. He yelled at us at times to stop arguing, but we ignored him. Darlene went downstairs so I yelled my final words after her. Darlene exited through the stair-well and I proceeded to finish dressing.

Shortly thereafter, Lamar suddenly barged into my bedroom. He hit me hard with his fist on the side of my forehead. My head slammed onto the hot water heater and Lamar yelled, "I'd rather do this than watch you go to hell." Shock and fear went through me.

I went downstairs after that. I didn't know what was wrong, but I was shaking badly all over. I started telling Lenora what happened and then I lost control of my words. I couldn't make a sound and appeared to be hyperventilating. Lenora yelled at Lamar for hitting me. Lamar ran to the neighbors for help. Everybody around me seemed frantic. My face shook uncontrollably as if a nerve had been hit.

The neighbor lady, Jennifer, took Dad and me to the hospital. I calmed down once I got to the emergency room. I sat on an examining table while Dad and the doctor argued between each other. He and Dad argued about Lamar's outburst. The doctor said Lamar was a violent twenty-year-old boy, and Dad said I had gotten what I deserved. Neither came to an agreement between each other.

The doctor spoke with Dad and me after deciding not to take any head x-rays since it seemed that I'd just had a nervous breakdown. Yet he told Dad to keep an eye on me throughout the night just to make sure I didn't have a head injury. Finally, Jennifer took us back home.

The house was quiet when we returned and it seemed like a strange day. Everyone took naps that afternoon while I sat on a chair wide-awake, alone, and worrying. Mom woke up when it was starting to get dark. She was confused and disoriented, so we had to tell her where she was.

Dad took me down to the basement and recounted every bad thing I had ever done. He wanted to make sure I got my share of the blame for Lamar's behavior. Nobody said anything to Darlene. Brother-in-law Joe stopped by to see what happened, and Dad told him his version of the story. Joe left and all was quiet again.

I went to church the next Sunday. I didn't feel like facing anyone so I spent a lot of time in the bedroom, which served as a nursery. One of the regular church ladies was nursing her child in the bedroom when she told me that she heard about the baseball that hit me in the head, hitting a nerve. Apparently, someone had told her that. I didn't bother to correct her. Why should I when nobody else told her the truth? I knew then that the facts of the story had changed. I didn't mind since the facts were unpleasant.

We had family fights, and some were rather major. Yet the story became forgotten as time passed on. Lamar was still a gentle-natured boy and I never saw another outburst like that from him. He remained gentle toward animals and humankind. He was a good boy deep down in his heart. I knew that.

Dear Journal,

I was with Ann today. I didn't pay much attention to her because I'm used to her being strange. I know there is something wrong with her and no one will fix her problem. We would rather be ignorant about the problems Ann has than to face the burden of intervention which goes against Amish traditions. We believe that being Amish in itself will remedy all problems.

I just wonder why I'm the one sentenced to care for her welfare. I've been with her every day for the last week. I know she starves herself but I didn't realize until today how scrawny she is. She pulled out her outdated portable tub. It's the kind of tub that Amish people in our community don't use anymore because we have bath rooms. Ann still doesn't have a bathroom.

I was busy cleaning when Ann called me to the little room where she was taking a bath. She needed a washcloth she had forgotten. I brought her the washcloth and I was shocked when I saw her bony legs as thin as sticks jutting out from her body. Like a moving skeleton she reached for the washcloth and said, "Danky".

She has kept herself inside her bedroom every day while I've been there and periodically calls me to her room to tell me what to do. She has kept Lillie in the bedroom with her at all times, never allowing her to leave the room. She wouldn't let me play with Lillie for fear that I would spoil her by being too nice to her.

I walked through her house dusting without any dust spray, just a dry cloth. I tried to cook for her although she never eats. I wait to walk home through the old dirt road every day just to get away from the sheer loneliness of her house.

I walk through the dirt road and ask myself, "When will catastrophe strike?" I'm worried, "Why should we accept Ann's fate?" I wonder what's happening at home after I worked through Ann's isolated house.

At Ann's house I watch the company of Amish people come and leave and in their concern and ignorance they always leave food. Ann won't eat the food. It always gets brought to our house and we end up eating it, unless Mom says its cooked bad and throws it away.

I remember when we took our trip to Virginia to see Ray and Ann. That was the longest trip we took as a family. My married siblings didn't come along. It was Mom, Dad, Teresa, me, and Darlene.

Our driver was an old friend of ours. We were all excited to travel so far and our driver was also excited. I remember, we explained to him that Ray and Ann were different. They had moved to Virginia to live extra plain.

They went beyond the Amish Ordnung and actually weaved their own material, talked about going back to covered wagons rather than having drivers and many in there community lived in tents. They had no batteries or motors and sheared their sheep for their own wool.

Most Amish people didn't think they were Amish anymore. They believed they were too plain to be Amish. I know our driver was expecting a cool experience.

We were in a shock when we came to Virginia and saw Ray and Ann's little shack. It was a hot August Day. Ann was wearing her black dress as usual. She wasn't allowed short sleeves in her Ordnung so she wore long sleeves. She had to wear a cape and apron at all times.

She was dressed in black from her neck to her toes. She wore a prayer cap that covered her hair entirely. She was only allowed a wood stove so the wood stove was burning wood in the middle of August while she cooked food. I knew she wouldn't eat that food. The tiny shack had furniture sitting along its wall, neck to neck. She made Ray spank her seventh month baby repeatedly, Yikes!

I shall never forget the look of shock on our drivers face when he saw her and her shack. He was completely appalled and we were taken aback, awkward.

I wonder many times why we're all so scared to intervene and try to help Ann. Her strange behavior and bad habits is a recipe for disaster. I've come to the conclusions that because we're Amish we're too withdrawn, internalized, and afraid to speak up. We are used to staying silent and accepting the doormat role. We accept all things bad and good without making the sacrifice for change. We have no courage and no strength to fight what is bad.

I will always wonder about her. I will always wonder about her children. I always wonder about her fate. I wonder what will happen to her in the end, in the very end when she's gone.

In sorrow I say good-bye forever, Regina

My Starving Sister-in-law

OUR BASEMENT WAS remodeled into an apartment when Ray and Ann got married. We painted the walls white, hung curtains in the window, and fixed it up as a home. It was clear that Ray didn't have the means to fully support Ann, and her family was too poor to contribute.

Ray and Ann owned a few nice things that he gave her during courtship; one was beautiful oak furniture. Still, Ray was not as financially successful as his brothers.

Time passed and eventually Ray built a house for Ann. They moved into it to live an independent married life of their own. It was a small, tin-roofed, unpainted house in the woods by an old, dirt road. It sat in front of an old forsaken graveyard with underbrush and scrubs decorating the yard. An outhouse sat behind the house. The inside of the house looked vacant with anything pretty hidden away, out of sight.

Her house was unlike any other Amish home in our community. Amish people in our community had refrigerators, bathrooms and running water. We could have modern conveniences as long as we didn't use electricity to operate them. Ann didn't honor or abide by that. She lived harsher than the *Ordnung* mandated and brought along her inner suffering as the cross she must bear.

Ann was a mouse-like character, reserved and submissive to the *Gelassenheit*. She almost never chuckled and only once did I see her cry. It was the Christmas when our whole family gathered together to celebrate the season and we realized that Ann's time with us seemed to be slipping away. It might be the last Christmas with her. She looked so skinny and peaked. We sang Christmas carols together, and Ann ran crying from the room.

Ann's mother died of cancer when she was only sixteen years old. She believed that she inherited the terrible cancer from her mother. She wore black dresses year after year, always in the wake of constant mourning, as she mourned the loss of her mother and many other family members.

An herbalist, Chinese doctor named Jill became a good friend of our family. She told Ann that she had cancer to convince her to take her herbs. Then again, Jill told everyone they had cancer to convince them to buy her herbs. The herbs didn't help Ann, and she suffered greatly from anorexia.

Amish people brought food for Ann but she refused to eat it, believing she was too sick to eat. Her menstrual periods stopped and she was sure she was going to die. She became so weak and skinny she couldn't work anymore. She would lie on her bed all day while at sixteen years of age I did the housework for her as her maid.

Weeks passed by as I took my daily walk through the old dirt road to work for Ann. Once I got there, I looked inside boxes and cabinets hunting for things that seemed to be hidden away. I cooked food for Ray as he tried to help at times

However much I may have tried to help Ann, I must say, that it's not an easy task to take care of a bedridden person. As a human, I struggled with the burden of it and it wore me out. I got tired of her dark little bedroom where she lay, fading away like a shadow in the darkness.

One night Darlene and I were washing the dishes. As we were doing this, we started joking around and laughing. I was taking a much needed break from caring for Ann as I had begun to wear down from the burden of that.

It was getting late when a knock sounded on the door. An Amish man, whose family had just left Ann's house stood at the door. He told us that they had just finished visiting Ann and she was having serious physical pain.

We all knew that we needed to go to her house and help her. That night Dad, Mom, and I went to visit Ray and Ann. My parents chose to bring me with them because they believed I could withdraw physical pain from people by using the power of the aura of my body.

Our family tried all natural and self-powered mind and body experiences for good health. Health foods and nature's way took over, including some questionable procedures from ancient times and traditions. Eastern medicine became a prime and became a big part of my teenage life.

My family also practiced mind power games to control the body. Innocent games we kids played were mind power games. In fact we children gathered our friends and demonstrated mind power by creating a circle and with the aid of a ritual we caused people to fall over at appointed times. We weightlessly lifted people and I learned more than ever before about the intense power of the mind.

This chosen lifestyle had nothing to do with us being Amish. Most Amish people are not naturally health-minded, but my parents and many of their close friends were.

Putting aside our healthmindedness, I didn't withdraw pain from Ann that night despite my attempts. We thought she was going to die. She looked deathly ill, lying still like a yellow-skinned skeleton. It was a pitiful sight to see her wasted body. I couldn't have helped her anyway. She needed nourishment, and I knew that.

Her bony face kissed her little, baby girl Lillie good-bye. Yet Ann was scared to die and lay in waiting. Ray faithfully sat by her side while Dad read a High German prayer three times, per Ann's request. As she said she could find no comfort and wanted to hear the prayer repeated.

Ann told Mom that she was afraid to die. She feared what death might bring. I am sure she feared hell due to her Amish upbringing. Mom told Ann that Amish people highly respected her. This was because Ann wore the longest dresses and biggest head coverings.

We finally got Ann's permission to take her to the hospital. Mom and Dad called a local Amish driver to take Ray and Ann to the hospital and they went along. I took baby Lillie home with me but I was worried when I got back home. "Would Ann survive and would Lillie be well?" I rocked Lillie and sang her a lullaby. I had that bad gutsy feeling inside that suggested Lillie was starved for love, especially after the aftermath of my own life experiences.

The nurses gave Ann a shot for pain in the hospital and the doctors did tests on her. The tests proved that Ann didn't have any serious illness aside from starvation. Mom and Dad came home to report that Ann seemed to be okay now and would stay at the hospital for a while. Ann stayed at the hospital and the nurses fed her intravenously.

We went to visit her at times and at one such time when Brother-in-law Joe was playing on his harmonica Ann went into a short-term, fifteen minute, coma. She never had another one and we didn't know what caused this one. Despite this, Ann became healthier. Eventually she was released from the hospital and even Jill had to admit that Ann's cancer was 99% in her head.

It was decided by my parents that Ann needed to move in with us until she got better. So Ray and Ann moved back in with us along with all of Ann's eating problems. She had many of them and restricted most foods from her diet and she also restricted Lillie's diet.

Tension was common with Ann around. This was especially true at the dinner table where no one focused much on food because we focused on Ann who ate almost nothing. Mom couldn't shut her prying mouth and would keep telling Ann, "Try the dessert, aren't you going to eat more food, you must be hungry in-between meals." She knew all along that none of her remarks persuaded Ann to eat more.

Ann had also breastfed baby Lillie before she had been admitted to the hospital. Breastfeeding eventually failed, though, because Ann's breast milk dried up due to starvation. Lillie lost so much weight that her hair fell out from malnutrition. We had convinced Ann to put Lillie on a formula. Ann did that and used glass bottles, so small that Lillie lost much weight from lack of formula. Still, after the hospital stay Ann kept many foods from Lillie and fixed yucky dishes.

Ann mixed all of Lillie's food together into a big slop at every mealtime. Medicine, potatoes, cottage cheese, meat, applesauce, became a blended, slopped, pureed heap. Who could stomach a meal like that anyway? I knew I couldn't and I couldn't blame Lillie for not wanting to. Rightfully, Lillie refused to eat the awful tasting medicine-food slop. Yet her parents slapped her in the face every time she refused to eat. We were all concerned for Lillie, who cried through every meal.

Teresa would sneak Lillie into the bedroom whenever she could. She would feed Lillie crackers in the bedroom that she kept hidden under the bed. We had to intervene with Lillie's feedings and we used the crackers to save her.

Yet no one suggested taking her neglected baby from her. Amish people simply did not consider or believe in doing this. As a young teenager, I couldn't do a thing. My parents might have been shunned had they tried.

I was worried about Ann's incompetence. She was clearly incapable of caring for herself, much less a baby. I was hoping to free baby Lillie from lack of love and protection, but now I knew I couldn't.

I would go to Teresa's bedroom every evening when it was bedtime. We would lie on the bed and listen to Lillie's cries. She cried every evening because her parents spanked her repeatedly for hours. Teresa would tell me she thought it would be better for Lillie to die than to be so mistreated. I would tell Teresa that I'd leave if things didn't improve. Than Teresa would tell me it was impossible to leave.

I'd think, "What does she mean, it's impossible to leave, think outside the box. Of course it's possible if we decide to make it possible, I don't see a big Mack truck blocking my pathway out."

Nonetheless, I hadn't left yet and I was not shielded from the dysfunction that surrounded us.

I became ill from stress and took to bed like a sore dog. I wanted everyone to leave me alone and let me disappear inside the covers of my bed. I dreaded when anyone entered the room and refused to eat at the table with the others. There was too much tension at the table. I always waited until everybody left the kitchen. Then I would sneak to the kitchen and eat in private.

I got terrible indigestion. My stomach became swollen and large and I was bloated during this time. I looked like I was pregnant. Mom would send me inside if someone drove past. She said she didn't want anyone to think I was pregnant. I preferred to stay inside my room where no one could see me. Every morning Dad came to my room to check my belly.

Ann came to my room one day and showed me a pretty dark red dress that the bishop's wife had sewn for her. I was surprised that the bishop's wife would sew such a prettily colored dress but I suppose even she got tired of seeing Ann wearing black all the time.

Through our experience with Ann we became a family of strangers living together. Mom often left for the day and Dad and Ray disappeared until mealtime. The rest of my brothers and sisters lived a secluded married life of their own. They stayed away during this time and some didn't even live in the community anymore. Darlene still went to school and this left Teresa and me alone with Ann and Lillie for a long and miserable day.

One day Ray beat one-year-old Lillie so hard that he left her bruised and wounded. He told others that he thought it was good for Lillie to get hurt like this. I had to confront Dad about this. Cruelty was criminal in my mind and I wasn't going to accept it. I went to Dad's tool shop and told Dad what had happened, hoping for help. Dad laughed scornfully in my face. He told me it was good for Lillie. "Lillie will not be spoiled," he said.

That day at the age of sixteen I left the tool shop in complete frustration. I walked to the house, worrying and feeling troubled. The pleasure my Dad got from brutalizing people and animals was my troubling worry. I couldn't tolerate his behavior and I couldn't make him see reason. Dad deserved to be in a prison, but he was above justice because he was Amish. Indeed, how could Ray and Ann justify their behavior, even for absurd reasoning? It blew my mind! What could I do about it, accept write it on paper?

Ann was spanking Lillie again hard and repeatedly, hour after hour one morning. She wanted Lillie to take a nap, after Lillie had a full night's rest and it was impossible for her to be tired. Ann based the fact that Lillie was tired on the fact that Lillie had cried most of the morning.

We knew why Lillie cried all morning. It was because her mother had hit her for accidentally touching the wrong thing. Little Lillie was the most well behaved baby I ever met. She was too terrified to behave badly. She barely breathed.

Teresa had enough of Lillie getting beatings that morning. She rushed to the laundry room and begged Mom to stop Ann from hitting Lillie more. Mom tried to tell Teresa that it wasn't that bad. Mom couldn't calm down Teresa so she decided to make an effort to stop Ann. She went to Ann's room and suggested that Lillie was hungry.

Of course, Mom's solution to every problem was food. She couldn't tell anyone that their behavior was cruel so she suggested food. After all it comforted her and prevented her from having to confront the uncomfortable truth.

The food didn't stop Lillie's crying. Ann suggested that Lillie had an earache and that I needed to withdraw pain. Lillie didn't have an earache, but I was good at pretending. I held Lillie and pretended to withdraw pain from her. Poor Lillie was so happy that I held her that she calmed down and completely relaxed again. I told Ann that Lillie had an earache just so Ann would be nicer to her.

The weeks passed in front of me with same nerve rattling abuse when one night I had the final straw with Ann. Lillie was crying far into the night and Ann was slapping her repeatedly. Hours were passing by and the slapping and crying wouldn't stop. A fierce bubble burst within my spirit. My mind told me I had enough and my heart felt it. So I loudly threatened to leave if things wouldn't change. Mom tried to quiet me for fear that Ray and Ann would hear me. I didn't care if they heard me. I thought it was time they heard me and I told Mom loudly and clearly.

I also started crying out of sheer misery for the situation which appeared unsolvable. Dad treated my crying as if it were abnormal, talking and shaking his head. He accused me of having an emotional breakdown and mental illness for crying.

I simply didn't want Lillie to be hurt, but they were only concerned about my tears. After talking with Dad I realized he was more concerned about the fact that the abuse bothered me than he was with the events of the abuse itself. This disgusted me.

Dad, Mom, and I went to see an unlicensed, non-Amish counselor while we dealt with Ann's anorexia. Ray convinced my parents that it was the right thing to do, as he thought we needed the counseling because of our issues with Ann. It was as if we were the ones who had the problem, rather than Ann having a problem.

I was chosen to see the counselor because of my crying about Lillie's abuse. Dad told the counselor I had an emotional breakdown. Therefore, I had the problem and not Dad. The counselor talked about my emotional breakdown like there was something wrong with me. It took Dad three minutes to convince a foolish counselor that everyone else was sick except him and Ann.

Of course, we didn't know that the counselor didn't have a license. We were Amish and therefore licensing meant nothing to us. He gave me a book while in one of our sessions called "Hide and Seek", by Dr. Dobson. I read the book and I liked it.

I was a tired and despairing soul hoping to change a situation with Ann. I couldn't find anyone to understand or listen to me in my despair. I decided to write a letter to Focus on the Family. I had the conclusion that the non-Amish world had problems. I perceived a spirit of open-mindedness about abuse in them. I found that refreshing, insightful and hopeful.

I will never forget how I had to sneak the letter to Focus into the mailbox. When Teresa questioned me about sending the letter, I lied to her about it. That is how scared I was to write the letter. My family would never approve of this. Living Amish, was supposed to be good enough.

Unfortunately, Lamar and Sue had a baby during this time. I had to be working at their house as a maid when Focus on the Family answered my letter. I didn't get to read it until later since I could not check my mail until I returned home from Lamar and Sue.

Teresa gave me the letter and watched me read it with disdain when I got home. She had opened the letter and read it while I was at Lamar's house. She was disgusted with me for lying about writing the letter.

Focus on the Family was sympathetic to my situation at the time. Yet a letter of sympathy does not change a situation. All in all, in the end, the letter didn't make my life better. Yet it was an effort on my part for improvement.

Mom decided that we didn't need counseling after two visits. After all, Mom's visit at the counselor was rather miserable with Dad blaming everything on her. He made it out as if he were the good guy. He accused Mom of nagging him, and he forgot that it had to do with his laziness. After Dad's accusations toward me, I didn't care myself since I had plans to leave the Amish someday.

Ray and Ann never changed their ways. I kept threatening to leave home if the situation didn't improve. This scared Mom, which served the purpose of my threats. She promised she'd resolve the problems with Lillie. She persuaded Dad to talk to Ray to resolve the problem, which he did. He told Ray that I was bothered about Lillie and he didn't want me to leave. He asked Ray to be more careful with Lillie.

The situation temporarily improved and the abuse was less severe. Ray and Ann moved back to their old tin home in the woods. Soon after, though, they were back to their old abusive selves. The good part was that none of us had to hear it anymore. The bad part was that no one was around to protect Lillie. I found that sad.

Later Ray and Ann moved to Wisconsin. They moved close to Mary and her family. My problem moved away and became Mary's problem. The abuse drove Mary nuts and she started counseling. She even made an effort to talk to Ray and Ann. The situation improved once more but then became worse yet again.

Ann never changed and left sad memories for the family to see whenever they came to visit. Memories of abuse and memories of starvation surrounded Ann. I wanted intervention for her, but the Amish people had excuses.

* * *

Darlene and I called the police in Virginia in the year 2002, after we'd left the Amish. The police paid Ann a visit and told us she was very skinny. They said she looked bad but she was starting to do better. I'm sure Ann herself told them this. They believed her because she was Amish.

I believe it's true that the police took Ann's side rather than Darlene or mine. His comments indicated lack of knowledge of the whole situation. So when the phone was hung up I realized that he would do nothing. It was as if an Amish story is forever believable, however false. Since nothing changed it became impossible to save her.

On February of 2003, Ann died, weighing forty-three pounds at her death. She left four children and a husband behind. Lillie was ten years and her sister, Rose was eight years old. The twin boys were five years old.

Our family knew that she was dying from anorexia, but the Amish people of Virginia gave her permission to die in her secluded world. Ann planned her death, exactly the way some people plan their life. Her friends and family believed she went to heaven.

She told Ray that she wanted him to marry shortly after her death. She told him who she wanted him to marry. Ray had a new girlfriend within two months after Ann's death. She was the girl that Ann suggested, and Ray married soon after Ann's death to start a new life with a new wife.

I never saw or heard much about his life after that. Mom told me that they lived in a better house and the children seemed to be doing better. I certainly hope this is true for the children's sake. Never again do I want to see such a heart-wrenching event.

The Witch of the Amish Community

WHEN I WAS sixteen years of age my family went to visit a Chinese, herbalist doctor named Jill. Dad learned how to do Jill's doctoring and he also taught others how to do it. He invited Jill to come for a visit after he learned how to do her treatments. Jill accepted his offer. She came to visit one summer, staying in a vacant house during this time.

My parents and their close friends believed Jill had extraordinary healing skills and power. I didn't know if she was powerful but I certainly was there for the ride. I was fascinated as I watched her standing like a porcelain doll, wearing expensive clothes, extensive jewelry, a wig, and heavy make-up. Her eyes were dark and mysterious making her looks almost frightening.

She had many statutes that she worshipped and her church was in her garage where she kept a half human, half dragon statue to worship. She brought her statues with her and prayed to her goddesses to heal our people. She was also the woman who had told Ann that she had cancer.

Mom, Dad and Jill performed the treatments on us, friends and family. They cut many small slits on our bodies, including genital area; with razor blades. They put many baby food jars with burning paper towels inside the jars on our skin. This left big, red blotches on our skin from burns. The heat from the bottles sucked blood through the slits on our skin, supposed to bleed out body poison. It was medieval treatment, called bleeding people.

Our family and friends performed this practice of their own free will. Our family had times when they wanted to use Eastern Medicine and natural resources, including psychic phenomena. Amish people don't have rules against natural health, although it's not their custom.

No, we weren't devil worshippers and didn't even agree with Jill for being a dragon worshipper. We believed Christ was God's son and we believed the *Ordnung*. Rather, we had a fascination with Wicca and the New Age that supported a natural source of health thought and practice. If this could make us happier and healthier than we believed we should use it.

We ate Jill's bitter tasting herbs and stinking potions. If we'd ask Jill what she made her herbs from, she'd say, "Chicken shit." Then she'd also call Dad "Chicken shit." We worked for Jill for no money and we paid her large sums of money for her chicken shit.

Jill told us that we needed to keep information about her to ourselves as people may have a problem with her. Yet one day an Amish woman, a good friend of ours forgot and told another woman about Jill after she got exited about Jill's skills.

This made Jill angry and she asked the woman, "Do you want the police to know about me and to put me in jail?"

Jill would tell everyone that she had a license to do what she did. She said, "Just because you don't see my license doesn't mean it doesn't exist."

She claimed that the President knew everything about her. She also claimed she had doctored Nancy Reagan's mother. Who knows, and why should we stop her? After all, Amish people could practice doctoring without a license.

Jill told one of her male patients that she could cure his epilepsy. She gave him one of her treatments, to cure him. I was alone in my room the following night after she gave the treatment. I heard the boy having an epileptic seizure while he was in the room next to mine.

Jill was angry the next day when she found out the boy had the fit after she had supposedly cured him. She told the boy that he needed to exercise, and then she kicked him in his shins. Everybody standing there laughed at the poor boy.

One of the Amish women came to visit Jill. She wasn't sure if she wanted Jill's treatments but she was considering it. Jill wanted the woman to have her treatments and she knew the woman was getting beatings from her husband. She told the woman that she wouldn't tell anyone about this abuse if the woman would just take her treatments. The woman got a treatment and her husband got away with domestic violence.

Social services came to check Jill's treatments. They had heard enough about cutting skin and bleeding to be alarmed. Dad and Jill talked to social services and quickly intimidated them. Jill told us children to tell social services that the razor slits were nothing more than little scratches. She refused to let social services see the treatments.

We children stood and giggled at social services while they observed us. We had no idea what abuse was and knew nothing about the law. We thought we were perfectly normal and it was our job to disown them. Since social services couldn't see the treatments and made no headways with Jill or Dad they left.

Jill gave us a hug when she was ready to go home. We had never experienced affection before. It was an odd practice for Amish people. Dad nearly whacked her in the back, being so uncomfortable giving a hug. After that our life continued to resume with our practice of bleeding people.

One day Mary's children were eating Jill's natural sugar. At least, that is what Jill called it. The stuff looked like crystallized, lumps of sugar. The children had a strange experience while they ate the sugar. Mary claimed that the children had a vision. I believe it was a hallucination.

The children said they saw strange snakes while they ate the sugar. The snakes were off-white in color and approximately three feet long. They were wide at the head and narrowed down to pointed tails. One snake crawled over the bookshelf where Mary kept her natural health books. The other snake touched the sugar that the children were eating.

Mary believed this was a sign that Jill was evil. She was the first one who had told us about Jill. Now she was warning us about her. Dad, Mom, and some others in the family didn't agree with Mary. They continued doing the treatments, but the others quit seeing Jill.

I wondered many times about the days of Jill's treatments. At times, I wondered why I hadn't left the Amish already. Nonetheless I believed my mother still needed my help and that the timing wasn't right, so I stayed.

Dear Journal,

I can hardly believe the year of 1993. It's a year that shaped my beliefs so profoundly. While I tried to decipher my values about the Amish, I have come to a conclusion about them.

I marked this year on my calendar because so many things have happened. First of all our community has decided they want to start changing the Ordnung because, as Father says, "We won't survive unless we become fairly modern or become very serious successful farmers again."

Not everyone in our community can agree that we should become a little more modern, such as the bishop and his family. They have decided to move to a new community that is just as plain as this one has been. A new bishop, his brother will take over our community with the new rules.

I'm glad because my dad had been running to the old bishop every night asking for permission to keep his saw mill more modern and the bishop kept making him remove all modern pieces from the saw mill. Dad is now 10,000 dollars in debt after removing all that.

Mom owns a successful bakery for the tourist business. We make thousands of dollars of profit a week now. It is so much fun but we get awfully tired of working in that bakery.

I get really tired of the tourists. We all do, but we can't run them off. After all, they are our survival and we advertise to them. They admire us so much.

Today a nice tourist lady approached us while we were shopping. She smiled at us with her camera in her hand. She reached out and shook our hand. She said, "I admire you Aae-mish, (She pronounced it with the long A sound) so much. I wish every one was as good Christians as you are, it must be nice living in a place of no crime."

We smiled politely and nodded and then continued our shopping. I could see the flash of the camera as she took our picture from behind us.

I got to thinking as she left, "What does she mean when she says "no crime"? She should meet my Uncle Bill because he opened a door this year. He started talking about the epidemic of sexual abuse in our community.

We have never discussed sexual abuse before this year. It has been a closed subject in our community. Uncle Bill doesn't like that and he has been talking about families that struggle with incest and rape. He has even gone as far as removing Amish abused children from homes, but the bishop has shunned him now for doing all this. He even made Mom and Dad make a church confession for listening to Bill.

We didn't get so fussed over sexual abuse until cousin Susan said she had been date raped by one of the Amish boys, Carl. The boy had to make a church confession for having premarital sex, but that was it. The rape was not mentioned and no one bothered to help Susan, despite the fact that other Amish girls have also accused Carl of raping them.

Susan sat in church after the rape and pulled a pin from her dress. She opened up a church song book and punched words in the book with her pin. She wrote, "I'm all screwed up." Oh boy, did she get in trouble for that.

Then a report ran through the community that an Amish preacher, my Uncle Sam had sexually assaulted a young girl. It was reported to Mariah, a non-Amish counselor and she reported it to authorities. He had to go to jail, but he resumed his preaching when he returned.

When cousin Magdalena's, children were molested by their Amish dad they brought them to our house for safe keeping. I don't think they were all that safe in our home, but it was a step towards recognizing abuse in our community.

The Bishop even talked to church members about sexual abuse and made it clear that it's forbidden. Yet so far most molested children have been sent back home where they're getting molested and the perpetrators only make lame church confessions. It doesn't stop them.

As I look across the church room I realize just how many of those children that have been abused. It's so many that it's quite startling.

I have come to a conclusion that Amish people have a lot of crime, but they just don't report it.

Well journal, I wonder if someday the Amish will have to deal with their crime. Dad says, "It's a sign that the end of the world is almost here". Maybe he's right because it's an outrage what I now know. Either way, the Amish recognize the abuse and just don't have the tools to deal with it.

After 1993, I have seen a bad flood in Missouri. I have watched an Amish community separate. I have seen my Uncle Bill almost everyday as he becomes more and more frustrated with the horror he finds.

When I see all this, it makes me wonder about the tourist lady we saw at the store. Journal I pray that we never have another year like this one. It's been crazy.

Good bye 1993
You opened my eyes,
Thank you, Regina

Times of my Amish Youth

I WAS NINETEEN years old and working hard in the early hours before dawn. Work didn't stop until after midnight as Mom's bakery frequently worked overtime. We didn't have breaks and we worked hard seven days a week. That consumed most of my teen years and left almost no time for fun.

I was Cinderella while I did my sisters' dirty work. I washed the dishes, day in and day out. We supposedly took turns washing dishes. It didn't matter because whenever it was any of my sisters' turns, they refused. Then Mom looked at me and said, "You do it." I washed the dishes because I didn't have a choice, and yet I was growing ever wearier.

Mom bought diet pills for us. A law passed that didn't allow people to sell those pills in stores. Yet a local Amish store stowed them in the back of their store and sold them anyway. Customers using the pills bought them as they desired.

The pills gave me lots of energy but not enough. I was still tired with an average of three hours of sleep a night. Yet I was still able to stay awake and do more work than the others when I took an over-dosage of diet pills. I lost forty pounds, weighing one hundred pounds and that made me feel better about myself.

We hired help for the bakery, but we all still worked too hard – except for Dad. We all worked hard to pay Dad's debt while he snoozed on the easy chair like a bum, with hired help doing his work. Mom took little catnaps throughout the day and we dragged onward in exhaustion.

We were just as chaotic and busy in the Amish world as the non-Amish world is. It was not at all as if we lived slow-paced lives. Our life was just harder to live, without as many conveniences. I learned that business is business regardless of religion.

We worked hard enough to make Mom look around for relief. She decided we would all feel better if we went to the local chiropractor, named Reed. She set up appointments for us to get chiropractor treatments. Our life became riddled with working our bakery, visits on weekends to the Kansas City Farmer's market to sell wares, and chiropractor visits.

One day Teresa started confiding to me after a chiropractor session with Reed. She told me how Reed was sexually assaulting her. She only told me about this and no one else because she trusted me as her confidant. Yet as time passed, I eventually decided that Mom should also know what was happening. After all, Teresa needed help. So I told Mom everything.

Now that Mom knew about the assaults she assigned me to be Teresa's protector. She made me go with Teresa to chiropractor sessions. That way, as a younger sister I could protect her from his assaults.

It angered Teresa that her younger sister was supposed to be her protector. It unsettled me that anyone had to go to Reed after what he did. I worried that he may possibly do it to me.

Mom said, "Reed is only after Teresa so you need not worry because Reed isn't after you".

I went to Reed several times with Teresa but I never had the chance to protect her. Reed would send me to a separate room from Teresa where he would begin his sexual assaults on me. Whenever someone approached the room he would quickly remove his hands and play innocence.

I pretended not to notice Reed's behavior. After all, what could I do? I was Amish and that meant I was a submissive girl. "The *Gelassenheit* means submission-yielding to higher authority. *Gelassenheit* entails self surrender, self denial and a quiet spirit."[7] A bowed head and a lowered voice replaced a proud face, and it also made me non-assertive and vulnerable.

I knew I was helpless with a Bishop who only shunned those who reported abuse. Besides Amish people have a myth that they can handle there own problems without the law. Technically, that meant no one would help me, anyway. Furthermore, it seemed Mom had it set up.

One day while Dad drove me home from Reed, I noticed his driving slowed down dramatically. It was as if he was contemplating a conversation. I was quiet as usual and didn't pay attention to him.

It was a rainy, summer day and I was feeling gloomy and worried about all those sexual assaults. I was not in the mood for a conversation with Dad.

Yet he started talking to me anyway, telling me about him and his older brother Levi. He told me about a time when he and Levi were small boys. He said he had a problem with his brother, Levi, because Levi was stronger than him. He never wanted his brother to win the fist fights, but his brother would always win because he was the biggest.

He said all my problems came from Darlene because she was physically bigger than I was and could win a fight between us. Despite Dad's claims, Darlene never bothered me and I had never given her size a moment of thought.

Now I had much more of a problem with Dad because I found him cold and unbearable. Yet, I couldn't tell him that because our heated conversation would never have ended. At the moment, he was irritating me with his conversation.

I finally made the mistake of telling Mom what Reed was doing to me. Mom stood over me glaring, yelling non-stop. She told me I had wanted this to happen and it was my fault. I had become a slut, a sleazy person.

The image of my cold, angry mother standing over me created a terrifying image. She stood their yelling and I knew she wanted me to take care of the situation myself because she didn't know how to take care of it. I didn't know how to take care of it either.

---

[7] Donald Kraybill in "A Quiet Spirit, page 20

Mom wouldn't send me back to Reed because I let her down, not protecting Teresa. Now Mom said Teresa could take care of her own self, after all.

She told Teresa to go back because she didn't want Reed to know we were aware of his inappropriate behavior. Somehow Teresa made excuses not to go back, and she never saw Reed again.

Now I lived in a nightmare that my mother had produced. Mom kept going back to Reed as if nothing happened, and Reed talked to Dad about sexual abuse as if he were against it. My father decided to believe everything Reed said.

We had plenty of troubles with Reed but we also had troubles with others in the community, including our neighbors. We had simple-minded neighbors living next door. They were our friends, dependents, and drivers.

One time Mom sent Darlene and me to the neighbor boy, Peter. We had to give him a message about a delivery. Darlene and I knocked on the door and waited for Peter to come. Peter yelled, "Come in," so we did. We stepped inside the door and waited for him.

Peter came to the door completely naked. Darlene pretended not to notice him, and I retreated rather fast. She calmly gave him the message and we left. We laughed all the way home because Peter was so fat we could hardly see his penis.

Uncle Bill made a big effort to stop sexual abuse in our Amish community. He gave up after much hardship, death threats, and cruelty from many Amish people. Amish men assaulted him, beat him, spit at him, and rejected him. They literally ran him from the community.

Amish people inside the community behaved like cornered, threatened, people. They were troubled with the idea of someone intervening in their life.

My own parents were not the type to talk to their children about sex. At least they didn't tell us until we were much older and already knew everything. They gave us naive sex books that an Amish woman wrote. It had less information in than what we already knew.

The woman writing the books was from a family of incest. She wrote about years of rape from her older brother. She blamed the years of rape on the factor that her brother witnessed animal sex. She had weird, obscure ideas about sex, not comprehending normal childhood sexual curiosity.

We definitely did not get a sex education in school. We shared information with each other, and that was adequate.

Now I suppose I could describe in detail each incident of sexual abuse, but I won't. It's a sore topic for anyone involved and in this situation I was involved. You see, I still see sex as a private subject and therefore in this particular time I will keep it private just like it was in counseling sessions after I left the Amish. I admit to its destruction but I know I have recovered.

This was the year 1993, a year in which I was very depressed. We had a terrible flood that year and the community fought bitterly. They fought over the *Ordnung*, which was becoming more modern. It caused moving and divisions in our community. And they continued to fight over sexual abuse.

I realize now that it didn't matter if we lied, stole, or cheated as long as we stayed Amish. An Amish teenage girl would get pregnant and we were told, "At least they're still Amish." I wouldn't put up with that belief. Of course, my leaving put me in an uncomfortable situation of being shunned, but I expected that and it wouldn't stop me.

After my conversation with Teresa in the kitchen about leaving the Amish and going through an unwanted Amish baptism, I was ready to leave now. I had seen my sister-in-law, Ann suffer and had given her all the help I could. I had exhausted myself trying to help Mom in her bakery.

On a warm day in August I realized that Mom had paid all of Dad's debt and was financially secure. She could survive without me now. I had endured enough troubles in this world, the Amish world. It was time to experience my new world. I ran away in the night and the next morning I began my new life.

Tell Mom I'm sorry for disappointing her.
Tell Dad the same.
I must confess that I believe differently now.
I have tasted the worst and the better of two different worlds.
It's an experience I needed to learn.

It taught me happiness.

Those Bothering Troubles

MY FIRST HOME away from home was very different from that of my childhood. Bob and Penny lived in a very nice modern home. They owned more vehicles than I could imagine and had an indoor and outdoor swimming pool with expensive accessories and luxuries. Although they said they weren't rich, they seemed rich to me.

I knew by now that Jacob (Ann's counselor) was not around. He was in jail for sexually abusing a client. I also found out that he didn't have a license to be a counselor. Penny discovered this after living in his neighborhood until he was arrested.

The first thing that Penny did was let my parents know where I lived. Mom and Dad brought out my few personal possessions to me so I could have them. They visited shortly, curious about my new beliefs.

On this visit, Father told me that he disapproved of a religion that required a person to be submerged in water to be baptized. He asserted that a sprinkling was good enough. I didn't offer to explain any new beliefs, which I had not yet deciphered. Otherwise he didn't appear angry and was nice to me.

In fact, Mom and I ate out and went shopping together, never discussing our differences. I thank God for that because it was an important time for me and I needed my mother's kindness more than ever. I realize that, compared to many others who left the Amish, I was living well.

Mother seemed rather anxious at times and according to my sisters she cried often and loudly, but never around me. She was pleasant to me during this visit and many visits thereafter.

It was apparent that if I wasn't going to be Amish anymore, then I would need to learn to live life successfully in my new world. If I failed, my family would be the first to notice and rub it in. I didn't need that.

Penny had taken me into her home and literally adopted me as her daughter, and she expected me to perform according to her expectations. She intended to teach me success in this new world. She was an educated lady and held to a high standard of performance by which she held me accountable as well.

The first month after I left the Amish was a month of adjusting. I was learning a new way to live and Penny showed me how to do it. It wasn't hard to do things the modern way, but Penny wanted me also to hold my head high and appear educated. I wasn't raised like that and it didn't come instantly or easily. When I did it wrong she would thoroughly scold me.

After the first month of living with Bob and Penny I got a job in a nursing home as a housekeeper. I also started working on attaining my GED and moved into my first apartment. It wasn't any form of high society but it was a step towards becoming independent.

I lived in a small old-fashioned, furnished apartment. My brothers and sisters paid me visits at times. Some visits were pleasant and others not quite so pleasant. Yet I frequently became lonely when I was alone in my apartment.

I didn't have a car or a television set but I was still very happy with what I had. I was happy for a change and I was gaining more independence and freedom as time passed.

I still saw Bob and Penny on a regular basis but our relationship was not as good as it had been in the beginning. I disliked their church because it was a small church with only married couples in it. The church only had six families in it and it was the same six families as it had thirty years ago when it first started. I was the only single girl going to this church so I stuck out like a sore thumb.

It was unknown to me that Bob had a history of making sexual advances on other girls in the church. While I lived in his home he was appropriate. At times he seemed too ornery and appeared a little dislikable but not to an alarming extent. Furthermore, I mostly stayed with Penny, who watched me more closely and preached a higher education to me whenever she could. I will always be grateful to her for instilling that knowledge.

One night our small church group left in the church van for an event. Bob took me by surprise while riding in the van. It was dark in the van and he threw a coat over me so nobody would see him. He began to behave sexually inappropriate to me, rubbing his hands on my thighs. I was quite flustered with him because he was the pastor of the church.

I also started having a relationship with a young man, named Isaiah during this time. He was someone I knew and met at my job. I never told Bob and Penny about Isaiah because I had no reason to do so – until this incident. Bob was making my life difficult and I wanted him to know that my interest lay in someone other than him.

I waited until we vacated the church van, and I told Bob and Penny about my relationship with Isaiah. I cared a lot about Isaiah and I was losing my trust with Bob. Yet, Isaiah was black and Bob was terribly racist. He hated black people and he yelled at me for being with a "nigger." He told me that black men smelled bad and would forever destroy my image. But I had no image to lose and color mattered none to me.

Bob drove to my apartment one night to pick me up. I was planning to go to Penny's and his house for a visit. I was ready to go to the car when Bob emerged from the car and invited himself inside my apartment. I asked him what he wanted but he never answered my questioned.

He kept grabbing and hugging me, taking me by surprise. When I went to the door to leave the house and go to the car Bob stood, barring the doorway. He suggested that I have sex with him, talking endlessly about beds and pillows waiting for us. I reminded him that he had a wife, but he ignored me.

Bob kept asking me repeatedly if I would have sex with him. I didn't know how to take his annoying advances but I kept telling him I wouldn't. Bob finally gave up and we went to the car to leave. He kept grabbing me repeatedly on the way to his home. I was unnerved but chose to ignore him. Things came to a rough halt soon after this experience, though, and I will never forget it.

One warm, sunny day I jumped in their swimming pool. I was enjoying the swim when I noticed Bob kept coming back to watch me. I thought his behavior was rather odd. After all, Bob was a very religious man. He always said he was too modest to see a woman wearing a swimsuit. He said his religion taught him to dress in strict attire. Bob and Penny always dressed very plain, which conveyed a serious belief in this statement.

Eventually, Bob came over to the swimming pool and leaned over the side of the pool, motioning for me to come to him. Thinking that he wanted to tell me something, I proceeded towards him. When I got close enough to him he grabbed my bra strap and pulled me close to him with the strap.

He held his face close to mine and asked me if he could swim with me. I became unnerved and my inner alarm went up. I backed away and told him no. He left and it appeared as if his game was over.

Penny came walking to the swimming pool shortly after Bob left. Apparently, she had confronted Bob and he had denied doing anything to me. Penny was sure that Bob was lying because she had seen him grabbing my bra strap. For the first time, I saw Penny light up in anger while confronting me, lashing out with accusations.

By Penny's accusations, I had become I had become a seductive slut, a flirt. She told me I deserved everything Bob did to me. It made no difference that I did nothing to cause it.

I was numb, emotionless and hurt for the rest of the day. The teachings of my background gave me no confidence to defend myself. I learned to stay out of the way when things were bad because I had no voice. I had learned this along with the *Gellasenhiet.*

I left the swimming pool that day, defeated. I thought, perhaps Penny should be glad I readily turned away from Bob's advances. It didn't matter because Penny wasn't in the mood to reason and Bob was uncooperative.

Bob yelled at me that afternoon for not being a better liar, telling me, "My wife would know nothing if you knew how to lie." I had no reason to lie. I wasn't making sexual advances and I didn't appreciate his advances.

I worried the rest of the afternoon about Bob. I decided I couldn't rest until I had talked to someone. My mind tormented my spirit and I wanted to resolve my problem, bringing peace to my mind.

I sat alone in my apartment after leaving Bob and Penny that day. I picked up the phone and called friends, Ed and Marsha. I knew them from Bob and Penny's church. I told them I needed them to come to my apartment for a talk. Shortly after this phone call, Marsha called back. She told me they were very busy and needed to cancel plans to come to see me. She said that they had called Bob and Penny to come over to talk to me. "After all," she explained, "Bob is the pastor of the church."

I became frantic when I found out that Bob and Penny were coming to see me. I knew the problem would not be resolved with Bob. I explained to Marsha that the problem was about Bob and Penny. They were the last people I wanted to see at that time.

Marsha was aware that Bob had made sexual passes to girls in the church. She sensed that I was seriously troubled about Bob. She promised to be right over to talk. Unfortunately, Bob and Penny were already aware of the problem also. They were planning to come as well.

I was sitting in the darkness of my living room when Penny arrived looking very quiet and angry. Shortly afterward, Ed and Marsha came, and then Bob arrived, filling the room with tension. I said very little about what happened, while Ed and Marsha heaped accusations on Bob, to which he made excuses.

It was a long, exhausting evening. After a cold, tense conversation, everyone went home. I went to sleep that night alone and troubled, knowing my life was chaotic. I knew things had become a mess but just didn't know what to do about it. Had I made a mistake by saying something? I didn't know, but Bob and Penny said it was a mistake, calling it an "unnecessary intervention." I wondered if they were right.

One of the other young women from church named Leah also complained about Bob. She had endured unwelcome hugs and kisses from Bob. She also decided it was time to confront the situation at this time. With two of us complaining, the problem could no longer be ignored.

I wrote a complaint to the hierarchy of the church. Two men of the hierarchy came to give me a short visit, also talking to Leah. They recorded everything we said on tape. They told me Bob would have to stop preaching.

The church requested Bob to get help for his problems. They believed Bob's behavior was inappropriate. They also believed he had various sexual encounters with other young girls. Bob refused to get the help the church requested. He was very angry that I got him in trouble and reminded me frequently. The church had many angry disputes over Bob's behavior, usually ending with angry emotions.

The time came when the church divided. Another preacher started preaching in Bob's place. Bob and Penny still tried to keep a distant relationship with me, usually to turn me against others in the church. It made me lose interest in the church and religion. After all, it served no good purpose for me.

One of Bob and Penny's daughters left the church in anger. The other daughter continued to go to church because she disapproved of her father's conduct. I left the church and gave up on religion. I didn't have the stability or desire to endure the instability and hypocrisy of this church and its religion.

This was my first negative experience since I had left the Amish. It was my first experience that taught me how the non-Amish Christian world had the same problems as the Amish. I wanted to see a better side of it.

Love and Troubles in a New Environment

THE FIRST JOB experience I had after leaving home was in a nursing home as a housekeeper, as I attempted to do things the modern way. Much of the cleaning was familiar to me, but I still disliked it.

My boss didn't help my "sorry" job at all. She sat at her desk all day with her suit and tie calling, "Regina, come to the office now." Usually she found something wrong with my work.

"You used to be Amish," she'd say. "You must know how to be a very hard worker, and we expect a lot from you".

I thought to myself, what a conniving bitch! Was she trying to take advantage of me because I used to be Amish? After all, it seemed to me that I was already working "dog-hard."

Yes! I knew how to be a hard worker. I just couldn't stand her and her laziness. Nobody likes working to exhaustion, and personally I hated the job and wanted to do much more with my life than clean up after other people.

My job hit a climax as all bad jobs do. Exhaustion hit exasperation and exasperation hit tears. Tears marked the end of a distasteful job which I then quit, and to this day I don't regret it.

That was an uncomfortable experience along with a few small events to convey that I was shunned. One such time was when Dad brought over an Amish preacher for a talk as the bishop requested. Dad hardly said anything and the preacher criticized and asked a few questions.

He asked, "Will you go to hell when you die?" I answered, "The judgment isn't mine and you should leave it to God."

He asked, "Did your honorable Amish grandma go to heaven when she died?" I said, "Leave it to God's judgment. It's not for me to judge."

He couldn't come up with any more questions for me so I was able to point out that we had a difference of belief which we would never agree upon, and I needed to go to work. That was the end of that event and it never happened again.

Another event was when Teresa married a widower who had five children. I will never forget her wedding because I was not invited to it.

She was afraid to invite me because I was shunned but I got a call from Brother Joe and he told me he had made arrangements for me to come to the wedding.

The neighbor boy Peter came and took me to the wedding and it was an expensive ride, costing much. I couldn't eat with my family at the wedding because I was shunned.

Instead, I sat at a table filled with shunned relatives while grandpa visited with me through the entire wedding. He was very confused and didn't know who I was due to his dementia but it was the best visit I'd ever had with him.

I had given my family twenty years of my miserable life already. I wanted them to leave me alone now and leave me in peace. I needed a chance to experience a good life. I needed to know the burdens and happiness of my own choices. Furthermore, I needed to experience love and freedom from condemnation. One such example was the condemning letters from Ray, but I learned to stop reading them and throw them away. I wanted to get rid of all its negativity.

It seemed to me as if I was always climbing a mountain, and the mountain was always crumbling underneath me. Yet I kept going in sheer determination anyway. I kept telling myself many times that life would get better. I had left the Amish and I knew I would have difficult moments after I left them. I knew I was experiencing normal life but at times it seemed too much.

My beliefs in my burdens vanished when I noticed charming Isaiah. The first time I saw him was at work. Isaiah leaned casually against the doorway, asking me if I was free for the evening. I wanted to know him and I found him irresistible. My thoughts wandered all afternoon, knowing I'd go home with him.

It was a slow and rainy afternoon when I went home with Isaiah. We got lost somewhere in hours of lovemaking. I lay wrapped in his arms while we watched movies and had dinner, together. It was as if we had always known each other. Morning seemed an eternity away.

Isaiah cooked dinner for me many times after that when I went to see him. He also spent money and time on me. The boat of time and distance seemed to rock on our side. Days slipped into weeks. Weeks slipped into months while we had wonderful love affairs and cozy moments.

During this time I got another job as a nurse aid. Isaiah started taking me to work every morning and I went home with him after work. We spent our daily life together with my new job treating me much better.

I fell in love with Isaiah but realized as time passed that he had problems with addictions and insecurities. He began to use drugs as an outlet for him. So in order to relate better to him, I also started using drugs. I snorted and smoked speed whenever Isaiah did. It helped me lose extra weight that I had wanted to lose, which made me feel better about myself.

One night Isaiah and I were drinking a lot. It was getting late and I was drunk. Isaiah wanted to have sex with me, but my head was spinning. I felt deadly tired and I wasn't in the mood to have sex. I told Isaiah I wasn't in the mood for sex.

He ignored me and started to have sex with me anyway. Perhaps he hadn't heard me. I tried again while telling him I was very tired and just wanted to sleep. He told me to give him more time and continued his thrusting.

I waited a moment until I realized he had no intentions of quitting, I panicked. I kicked Isaiah from me and he reluctantly got off, cursing. I turned away from him and lay still with my eyes closed, pretending to sleep. I tried to clear my head but it was hard.

It was a long night, and morning seemed an eternity away. Time seemed to stand still. Nonetheless, I had a new job, and work had to be done the next day. I got up in the morning and went to work, trying to put the incident behind me. I had to forget the incident. After all I still loved him.

My second job was playing in a good favor to me. The minimum wage increased a little and I got experience being a nurse aid in a place where I didn't need a license. This experience helped me prosper more and set me up for more opportunities in life.

It was a small beginning of becoming more financially secure. I got experience working with psychotic and mentally ill patients, with life bringing all the cursing, mumbling, and dopiness that come with mental illness. I enjoyed taking care of my patients, but I had many long days and nights at work.

The nurses believed that ghosts lived in the retirement home. The administrator's office was supposedly haunted, and it was called "The death room," having been used previously to keep dying patients.

One night when I arrived at work one of the nurses claimed she saw a ghost. She said the ghost was a little girl who had died in the death room. She saw the little ghost carrying a mattress across the hallway to the office. It was during a time the office was unoccupied while the administrator was out on vacation.

I never saw a ghost in the retirement home. Still, I had chills as I worked alone on the second and third floor. I had a constant urge to look over my shoulder to check my terrain. It didn't help that patients had nightmares, often walking and talking in their sleep.

I was working at this job when I found out I was pregnant. The landlady made me move out of my apartment when she found out.

She said, "The rental agreement states that only one person can live in the apartment, your pregnancy creates two."

So I moved from my apartment into a new apartment in a Southern-style mansion-like house. I loved the big white pillars on the front of the house, which reminded me of the old South.

I lived in the "attic area" of the house. The apartment was in dire need of repair and maintenance, being very rundown. I repaired many things on my own, preparing for my baby. The landlord was very slow in any effort to fix the apartment, despite state laws.

I spent long nights working with morning sickness. It bothered me whenever I came to work on the night shift. Therefore, it became night sickness and caused me weariness through the night. I would periodically go to the bathroom for little catnaps and nausea spells.

The hardest part of my job was carrying heavy laundry baskets. I had to climb up three flights of stairs with each load so I asked the administrator for a work change. As a punishment for asking, she added more work to my job. Now my job became a tremendous burden.

It became easier as time passed. My workload increased but my night sickness left. I enjoyed my job more when I was feeling well enough to work. I planned on working until my due date, putting my heart into my job.

I had one obstacle at work to deal with. It was a big, fat kitchen employee with a mouth as big as her frame. She was prejudiced against white women dating black men. She made it well known that she hated Isaiah because he was black. How I dreaded her presence and her rude comments!

She would say ignorantly, "You know, I'm not prejudiced against niggers, I just can't stand them." I wanted to tell her she was stupid but I didn't have the emotional strength to fight with that intimidating woman.

My supervisor laid me off along with a number of other employees in November. It was one month before my baby was born. I filed for unemployment to secure income until the baby came. I began to prepare for the birth of my baby while enjoying a few wonderful baby showers in which I received beautiful gifts. I also worked hard to finish the maintenance in my apartment.

I had become friends with one of the employees at the retirement home. We spent many days together that last month of my pregnancy. As we sat together talking, I received bad advice from her about getting on welfare. I believed she knew more than I did so I did a major fraud during this time to get on welfare. I lied about a chunk of money I had at the time. After the fact, I lost all the money on my fraud through blackmail to her, regretting my decision. I realized too late this decision was stupid.

I didn't tell Mom I was pregnant for five months. Then I only told her I was pregnant because I couldn't hide it anymore. I didn't need her concern or worry any earlier than necessary. I wanted her support.

I waited until she made one of her little visits to my house, and then I told her. I was lucky to have a mother who was quiet, respectful, and pleasant when she received the news.

I didn't need to tell Mom I was pregnant, though, because she already knew. Leaving the Amish made me a target of gossip. Everyone from the small town I lived in all the way to the Amish community already knew it. Everyone was good at making everyone else's business their business, which was something I couldn't appreciate.

I saw Isaiah infrequently throughout my pregnancy. We were not lovers anymore during this time. I also quit using street drugs in protection of my baby. He had given me the freedom to choose abortion or life for the baby at the beginning of my pregnancy. Now he was angry that I hadn't chosen abortion.

I saw Isaiah again when I was six months pregnant. We went to McDonald's for breakfast and argued the entire time we were together. He still wanted me to have an abortion. I didn't have the heart to have an abortion, and it seemed cruel and unreasonable. Furthermore, I felt I was an adult in an adult relationship wanting to keep my baby.

Isaiah came driving past one day when I was nine months pregnant. He stared at my pregnant belly. He stopped in to see me a few minutes later. It was the last time he came to see me before the baby was born.

I wanted to talk to him but it became too difficult to do that. The property owner stood between us, yakking the entire time. Isaiah finally attempted to leave and went to the door. I ran after him and we exchanged a few words. I asked him where he was going and he shrugged his shoulder. Than he left, out of sight.

On December 8, 1998 my beautiful, black-haired baby girl was born. Isaiah was nowhere with me. He left town at this time while running from all his responsibilities, leaving me and the baby behind. When he left I missed him very much, wishing he'd come back.

I brought Penny, Mom and Darlene with me to the hospital when I was in labor and Penny was quite irritated when she discovered that only one person was allowed in the delivery room, especially when I chose my mom to stay at my side through the delivery. It was Mom's special moment to hold my hand, cry and give me ice chips and she did all that. She held the baby even before I did after she was born. I was a little jealous but I was glad to have my mom.

I also thought that nourishing and caring for my baby would bring me all the fulfillment life could offer. Furthermore I believed I would be fulfilled enough that I wouldn't desire a romantic love life after her birth. Yet I was still emotionally attached to Isaiah, and these feelings stirring within me prevented me from forgetting him.

Yet I still believed I needed to focus on being a mother. In fact I meant to enjoy mothering to the fullest. After all I loved babies.

Dark Moments in Hard Places

I HAD A lot of time now since I wasn't working a job. So I often sat in front of the television with my baby in my arms, not doing much. One day passed into another while the sun came up and the clouds went by. My baby slept and cried while I waited for better times. Sometimes it became better until the natural cycle of life changed things for the worse.

I loved my beautiful baby, but I still experienced postpartum depression after her birth. I was also bored from being all alone with a little baby and having no other social life. I wanted a good job, friendships, and the love of her father who had abandoned us.

Many of my hours of boredom were spent talking on the psychic hotline, amusing myself. As I talked on the hotline I got much information from the psychics.

I began to learn about events surrounding Isaiah. It was information that was important to me since I couldn't find it in my heart to let him go.

"*Isaiah is living in Texas in a drug house. He doesn't know that undercover cops are coming to the drug house on a regular basis acting as part of a drug gang.*

One undercover cop is a woman with red hair. Two of the cops are men with brown hair. They are waiting for the right time to take action, and they will either kill or arrest Isaiah.

Isaiah lives with a dark heart and a cold soul and he is surrounded by evil people. He is in danger but doesn't realize it. He doesn't know that the undercover cops will kill many people when they expose themselves. It's hard to tell if Isaiah can get away but we believe that someday Isaiah will return to you. He will show his feelings more than ever".

These were the words of the psychics. Little did I realize how true these words would become? Most people think that psychics make up everything and I didn't believe them myself until I saw the evidence. Only time into the future would expose the truth.

One of the most important pieces of advice came the last time I talked with a psychic. She advised me to talk to a counselor and a preacher. She also told me that God loved me and that I needed to start praying. Perhaps she had a spiritual heart. I don't know, but I learned with time that she spoke the truth.

The things unknown to me was a factor that created fear in me, which is why I relied on psychics. It comforted me to listen to them and calmed my fears. Furthermore, the wrong things happened to me at the wrong time, like the way my money ran out at the wrong time which was shortly after the birth of Destiny. This made me even more reliant on psychics.

I was left with problems that didn't have quick or easy solutions, like the unwelcome visit I got from Ray one day when I was alone in the house. I ignored his knocking, pretending I wasn't at home. The good things I desired seemed an eternity out of reach, like the vehicle I needed for transportation. Time crawled while I waited for important things to happen, and those important things didn't happen.

Evermore I kept my faith while knowing that the cycle of life changes and eventually become better. It was the one thing that gave me hope. I prayed often and thought of the improvements of my life.

I thought I'd be a strong Mother who could handle anything but my baby girl Destiny was very difficult to breastfeed. I wanted to be focused on being a full-time breastfeeding mother but my breasts produced too much milk. They began to hurt a lot from engorgement. After months of dealing with bleeding nipples and discomfort, I gave up nursing her. She was four months old and it seemed much too soon to stop, but it seemed the better choice.

My mother and sisters came to visit whether they were invited or not. Darlene usually watched TV when she came to visit, and Mom would hold the baby. Sometimes we went on walks or shopping trips together. I couldn't even tell that they shunned me.

Yet the visits outstayed their welcome and every visit was followed with an invitation to come back home. Still, I found it too difficult to tell my own family that they were a burden to me

My mother was glad I had a baby, even though I was a single mother. She kept telling Darlene this every time she came to visit. She'd ask me if she could take the baby home with her and have me pick her up in a few weeks. She always hoped that she could lure me to come home as well. It frightened me that my mother would ask to take the baby, and I never let her.

I knew I had problems after leaving the Amish, such as experimenting with street drugs and then becoming a single parent. I also had problems before I left the Amish with abuse. Yet my family never discussed my abuse and weren't aware that I had tried drugs. They were already used to seeing Amish unwed mothers in their community so that didn't seem to faze them either. They simply wanted me to be Amish again.

This caused me a lot of stress and my brain suffered from exhaustion. I tried to commit suicide twice the first month after I had my baby. I failed at both attempts and temporarily ended up in the mental hospital until my suicidal streak left. In my mind, I was the victim rather than the conqueror. I should've been focused on my baby, but I only saw my problems in my immaturity.

I knew I had to get out of my house and make efforts to live again, to snap out of my depression. My problems and immaturity caused me start dating again as a way to live. I started dating Todd as I gave up the idea that Isaiah would ever return.

Todd was a highly experienced lover and held a high aura of excitement. He was flashy and fast-paced – too much to handle really. Todd was also an ex-con from Kansas City. He was heavily involved in using and dealing drugs.

I would sell food stamps to Todd in exchange for methamphetamines. I also did cocaine and marijuana. I received enough speed for myself to use and sell the spare amount.

I started having friends over for nightly rendezvous of sex, drugs, and alcohol. I had affairs with other men whenever Todd was not around. I simply didn't care while I was high. It was the beginning of a promiscuous lifestyle for me.

I also lied, cheated, and shoplifted on a regular basis. I lost myself in a dark world where problems seemed impossible to cure. Furthermore, I now had social workers in my life because of my suicidal background.

My problems were severe enough to make a social worker decide I needed to move to the city so I could go to college and pursue an education. She also wanted me to move away from a town that was prejudiced and my invasive family.

Another social worker came to see me shortly thereafter. Someone reported that I was on drugs, drinking, and neglecting the baby. She immediately discovered that the baby was doing very well and was far from neglected. In fact, she said the baby was spoiled from getting too much attention. I don't think Destiny was spoiled but I did play with her a lot.

She told me she would dismiss the report if I would move away in two days and get out of town. I decided to move because I had drugs in my system and I didn't need her to know. I couldn't afford to lose anything, especially Destiny.

So far after leaving the Amish I had made troubling choices. As I saw the choices I had made, I realized that I needed to start over and do better. I also needed to see more of the good side of the non-Amish because I knew it existed on the "right side of the tracks".

I made it through this period of my life through my realization that no easy way existed anywhere. It had not existed in my childhood, and it didn't exist in my first job away from home. It did not exist in my first serious relationship or as a new Mom. I could make a new beginning.

Many Moves

AT THE AGE of twenty three I moved to St. Joseph, Missouri as the social worker requested. It was not the best of circumstances but I had to save myself and now I had my chance. When I arrived there I moved into a homeless shelter because I had no other place to live. I also started college the same day. Of course I brought my baby with me, put her into daycare and paid for college with a government grant.

A nice college professor thought it was awful that I lived in a homeless shelter while going to college. So she convinced me to move from the homeless shelter to a Women's Abuse Shelter, the YWCA. I moved there the following night. Yet it was also uncomfortable living there as a mother and a college student. So I began to look for yet another place to live.

As I looked for another place, an English college professor invited me to live in her home. I was happy she asked me and accepted her offer. I stayed for several months until I realized I was ill and ended up in the hospital.

The college professor decided she didn't want me to stay in her home after I became sick, because it was a burden to her. She asked me to move out, so I went back to live in the Women's Abuse Shelter again.

With all these problems, I decided my life was too difficult for schooling. So I dropped out of college to take care of myself and spend time getting healthier. I also found an apartment to live in.

It was in a black neighborhood with a high crime rate, the "hood". The crime rate had greatly improved by the time I moved there, yet it was still a "hood" with all its problems. Still, the scenery was rather pretty with oak trees and squirrels everywhere.

The most positive thing I did while I lived in that city was go to Beauty College to earn my cosmetology license. It gave me hope for my future as I dreamed of better times. I also needed to do something to improve my life now that I had quit the other college.

The worst thing that happened in that city was when I went out on a date, and that night I was raped by my date. I called a counselor the next day to report what happened. She said it was time to forget the incident, but I didn't know how it was possible to forget the rape so quickly. The trauma of this event caused me to fall into another depression.

Yet I was trying to get an education and I didn't have time to deal with it. I had to move on quickly in order to stay focused on my priorities. So in an effort to salvage some peace in my life, I prayed a religious prayer for salvation and that night I had a dream.

I saw a tall crystal shoe, as big as a building. On the bottom floor of the crystal shoe was a large church. It had a crystal stairway leading out through the top opening of the shoe, which served as the outskirts of the church. A crystal phone was on the wall of the shoe, by the crystal stairway.

I saw my mother walking on the crystal stairs but she stopped to pick up the crystal phone. I watched her make a phone call to Joyce Meyers, a Christian TV minister. As they talked on the phone Joyce ministered to her and than captured her in a sphere of crystal for the glory of God.

I awoke from this dream thinking about my mother. Could she ever be changed? I tried to visualize her leaving the Amish to become an outsider like me, but that was an impossible thought. I contemplated how it would seem if she were to become Mennonite, but that also seemed impossible. I imagined what it would look like if she chose to be New Order Amish instead of Old Order Amish, like she was now. That was a nice thought because then she wouldn't have to shun me anymore. Nonetheless, I doubted she would do that either. Fitfully, I went back to sleep and then had a much darker dream.

I saw a place of darkness, a place of dark spirits and abandoned children. In this place, I saw my mother sitting with a bunch of abandoned children on a small boat. All around me and her was darkened water and gloomy weather. It looked dismal.

Neither she nor I had much to say and we found little comfort in our circumstances. The children got no comfort and we had no way to appease them. Nor did we have the spirit left to try.

The knowledge of this dream didn't automatically appear to apply to my life, and I wasn't sure what it pertained to. Would I ever know what it meant? I probably would, but at that time I didn't know it.

I was troubled enough about my mother and the dream to start thinking long and hard about the way I was raised. I also thought about the prayer for salvation I had prayed earlier. Would that make a difference for me?

The prayer didn't make my life any easier or the days any better, so it wasn't making a difference. Religious churches claimed my life would get better through prayer, but they were wrong. I had addictions I couldn't stop, and it caused me problems regardless of any prayers.

I struggled to leave drugs alone and I was still disturbed by the rape. At times I relapsed and used drugs again. I also lost custody of baby Destiny for one week during this time while I pursued some therapeutic help. I worried every day until she returned to me.

I had a counselor while I worked on getting therapeutic intervention. He was also an attorney. He said that my chances of getting Destiny back were attainable if I admitted I had a drug problem and offered treatment for myself. He said a judge would just need to hear a plan for treatment.

I quit being promiscuous and went to Narcotics Anonymous as an appeasement to the judge so I could keep my baby. Social services were not in my life anymore. They believed I showed an effort to improve my life for better and that I was taking the right steps.

I will never forget the look on Destiny's face when she returned to me. She stared at me as if I had become a stranger. I felt like a terrible Mother and made a resolution to always keep her close and to improve everything in my life.

I kept going to Narcotics Anonymous and received counseling through that entire year. I tried my best to pull my life together for the good of Destiny.

Broken Dream of Love

I HAD WORKED on some college now and received some counseling. For a while I went to Narcotics Anonymous until I decided I didn't need it anymore. I still worked on my cosmetology license through all this and wanted to complete it. I was also miles away from my family now and attempting to live life independently.

I still missed the good times I used to have with Isaiah. I missed the way he used to cook and clean for me and the fun we had together. Most of all, I missed our melancholy moments when we used to listen to sentimental music early in the mornings.

Spring was a time for changes in my life. I was twenty four and Destiny was sixteen months old when I went to the local child support agency so I could collect child support from Isaiah. The child support agency had luck in locating Isaiah. He was transferred to Missouri and put in jail to wait out a court date, and a court order was made to collect child support payments.

Once the child support order was dealt with, Isaiah came to see me. We fell in love again and we made a decision to common-law marry and share our life together. During our marriage, Isaiah told me much about life in the time he was away from me.

I found out as he talked to me that he had lived in a drug house in Texas. He had seen undercover cops and he could describe each of them exactly as the psychics had described them to me earlier when I used to talk to them on the phone.

He spoke of a drug raid that killed many addicts the day he was arrested for child support. Isaiah had gone out to buy groceries and it had saved his life. The raid and the killings had ended by five minutes when Isaiah returned to the drug house. The police checked his record and discovered that he owed me child support, so Isaiah had been arrested.

At first things seemed good in our relationship. I watched Isaiah cook, clean and be a daddy. He washed dishes and played with his little girl, and I loved that. I listened to him when he talked about long term decisions for us. We often discussed commitments and made plans to officially and legally marry someday.

I found comfort in watching him stand over a stove frying steak and potatoes and cooking corn on the cob, while we discussed our life. He wanted to be a "stay at home" father, while I pursed a career. But what career should I pursue? I wanted to become a licensed cosmetologist but would that bring in a steady income? We weren't sure. Either way I was still in beauty school and I wanted to finish it.

So we decided we wanted to have four children for him to take care of while I worked. We spent hours walking along the street looking at houses trying to decide which one we liked. We discussed how we'd remodel and decorate each house. Those were the good times we had.

I fell in love with his flashy smile and adapted to his easygoing ways. I enjoyed being a wife, but I knew Isaiah had a dark past and I feared its effects. I didn't want him to bring his darkness into our marriage because I was in love with his good side.

Darkness was inevitable, though, because Isaiah was still possessed by his drug addiction. It was a problem that didn't show its face upfront but eventually evolved. Our happiness lasted until drugs reached our home.

It was a big difference when I first saw Isaiah walk up the sidewalk and flash me a smile. He took my hand to show me off in the neighborhood and I was happy. Than I saw how he was when he was high and angry and I began to feel a dislike for him. I wanted to be with him when I saw him smile on the sidewalk; it was beautiful. I didn't enjoy him when he was high and threatening me.

His drug habit became more prominent and his jobs grew fewer. It wasn't that Isaiah didn't try hard enough to find a job. He tried, but it was hopeless with warrants out for his arrest, warrants for all the people he illegally "ripped off." I used some drugs at times but not much because I was too preoccupied with Isaiah's problems.

Isaiah was a respiratory therapist but the only places he could get a job was at a car lot as a salesman. But he didn't manage to sell many cars as a salesman and therefore didn't make much money. He was in more trouble with his jobs than not, constantly obsessing over his drugs.

He began accusing me of taking more than my fair share of drugs. He quit cooking and washing dishes while often living in his own world of paranoia. We took many trips to Kansas City in search for his fix and it consumed our life.

One day he told me that nobody would know if he killed me because I was too isolated. He said, "You have no relatives around, and I don't know of anyone who knows you. I could kill you and not a soul will know." I began to fear him and wondered if he would act on his threat.

We were arguing one day when Isaiah started yelling in my face. I reached up to push his face away from me. He became so angry that he held the hammer he had been holding, over my head. He threatened to hit me with the hammer if I touched him. Well, I didn't touch him. I didn't dare.

Isaiah accused me many times of cheating on him. He also went through periods where he threatened to kill me. He told me I had to be careful or somebody would find me on the street, dead and bloody.

Isaiah didn't treat Destiny badly, though. At the same time, he was too obsessed with cocaine to notice her very much. I feared Isaiah's hostility, and I realized our home was unstable. I didn't know how to handle Isaiah because he was unpredictable. His feelings were hard to distinguish and left me guessing and worried. I then lost all sight of his good side.

Isaiah threatened to kill me more and more often, and he used up all our money on drugs. He'd promise to quit doing drugs and I'd want to believe him, but then he'd buy more. It was a struggle just to keep food in the house. I never knew how we were going to survive.

I had sacrificed to save money and he had the contempt to take it. I despaired and wondered when we'd crash to the bottom.

I would sit in the back bedroom on the couch, clutching my purse. I felt alone and insecure, and I was always afraid he'd take the last of our money. Isaiah found me where ever I was. He would promise to buy a car if only I would give him more money.

Isaiah did help me get my first car while we were together. I couldn't drive it because it was a stick shift, and the old car died in two weeks. Isaiah got another car and gave me my first driving lesson. This gave me hope that life would get better. I was learning something I longed to learn.

The driving lessons didn't last long because Isaiah got into serious drug dealing. He brought strangers into our house while selling cocaine. He refused to tell me what was going on. He acted as if it was none of my business.

I knew what was going on anyway because I used to sell drugs with my ex-boyfriend Todd. I wasn't innocent anymore and mistrusted his refusal to talk to me about his drug dealing. He was becoming more distant from me as the weeks passed.

I was very discouraged during this time. Our financial situation was completely out of control. I would sit alone in the house thinking about the occurring nightmare. I even quit doing drugs altogether because I was tired of Isaiah blaming me for taking too much. Yet none of this improved our relationship.

I had been going to church before we started our relationship. I quit going to church while I was in the middle of this messy relationship. It didn't seem to matter anymore with everything going wrong. I simply had to focus on surviving.

I was angry one day when I found out that Mike, a preacher we knew, had bought drugs for Isaiah. Mike was supposed to be our friend. He was supposed to be a positive influence on Isaiah, or at least I had hoped so. He was supposed to know the difference between good and bad, or at least I expected that from him. He had invited us to church, as preachers do. He refused to drink beer, believing it to be morally wrong, but he still damaged our lives.

Isaiah's threats were intimidating and he meant to carry them out. I learned quickly that it was better to let Isaiah have control rather than me. His behavior got worse when I was defensive. He acted as if he knew everything and I suffered in its darkness, too afraid to defend myself.

I called the house one day to find Isaiah stoned as usual. I told him to get his things and move from the house or I would call the police. He told me his death threats were a joke and I shouldn't take them seriously. An angry man making a death threat is an odd way to joke, and I didn't believe him.

He moved out that day. He knew I'd call the police if he didn't leave. I moved back to the Women's Abuse Shelter in an effort to be in a safe house. I didn't know if Isaiah would try to return to the apartment. In this catastrophe, I was forced to quit beauty school.

I can just imagine how impossible our life would've become had we been foolish enough to get a marriage license. Our happiness lasted for such a short time, and I could see a separation following us quickly.

Oh, yes, I loved him and I know he had strong feelings for me. Yet I realized, with common sense that love in itself is not enough. All the feelings of love in the world could not cure all our problems.

For all the times that I disapproved of my mother's marriage with my father, I had to admit that my own marriage was no better. I realized that problems existed in both worlds.

I still wish I were in love and that love was enough. I wish it were the same as it was in the beginning of our relationship. I still want a man with elegance, charm, and outgoing love. I want to marry that man and stay in love. It would be my true love story. Sometimes I think it could happen, but I know it only happens in a dream.

The Many Moves in my Search for Home

I WAS STANDING on top of a sloping hill admiring the valley below. It was such a beautiful, happy place with green pastures, brooks, and trees everywhere. I found it breathtaking as I took the time to drink in the sky and smell the fresh air. A peaceful, happy feeling flooded my soul.

I had just bought the most beautiful piece of land and was ready to have a very important building built there, maybe a house. As I stood there carefree and cheerful, I saw a shadow. I turned toward the shadow and suddenly my father stood in front of me with a look of rage in his eyes, glaring at me in a cold, spiteful way. He aimed a gun at me in pure vengeance. He stood there like a barrier trying to prevent me from getting the land I bought.

I woke up from my dream, knowing what this dream meant. My father had always wanted me to fail since I left the Amish. He had to prove that I was wrong and brings me back to the Amish. If he could prevent me from getting something, it would be all the more glory for him.

Regardless of his opinions I had a need to have a comfortable home where I could prosper without barriers, just Destiny and me. This belief and vision led me to dream about beautiful cottages, pretty pieces of land and a strange, frightening house.

I saw myself with Darlene and Destiny in a large, ugly house. Mostly I remember what the house looked like. It had many huge doors with cracks so wide we couldn't lock the doors. It had holes in the walls and rain dripping from holes in the ceiling. The largest room of the house had no floor, only grass, and there were gaping holes everywhere. It looked cold and miserable.

I patiently stayed in this house because God told me that if I lived their now, I could move where I wanted later.

I woke from this dream beginning to think about my future. I had to see a future past Isaiah and the abuse shelter. I also had to see a life where Destiny and I could survive in peace. I knew that perhaps it wouldn't happen as planned but at least I had to try.

I had a dream to move to Colorado Springs after previous times when I read Dr. Dobson's books. My dream became a destroyed plan because my finances didn't allow me to move there. I decided instead to move from the Abuse Shelter where I was staying and move to another Women's Abuse Shelters close to Kansas City. I didn't feel like I belonged there so I decided to move directly to the heart of Kansas City instead. This time I moved to a Homeless Shelter in Kansas City, as I worked on relocating there.

On any given day, I sat in the old alley outside the homeless shelter. The stone walls stood tall on each side of the alley with the shelter itself looking worn out.

These were the dangerous streets of Kansas City. Yet it didn't stop the staff from turning us out into the streets every day when daylight hit, locking me out on the street.

I'm positive that I need not phrase to anyone that streets are the most formidable, unfriendly place to stay. It offers no comfort and protection, and one morning I noticed Destiny coughing a lot. I spoke with a shelter employee to let her know I had a sick baby.

She was cold and indifferent and barely looked at me. She said, "You're late leaving the shelter, so you'd better leave now."

I left the shelter and the employee locked the door. It was pouring rain when I stepped outside. I stood in the alley to the wall, trying to stay out of the rain with my sick baby. She kept coughing a deep, congested cough. I didn't know she had bronchitis, but I was in no place to take care of her.

I cried and prayed that God would let something good come my way out of my homelessness. Sometimes I cried and prayed and hardly knew why. Yet I still kept on talking to God in all my hopelessness. I was completely desolate and worried with no home to take my sick baby, and it seemed as if no one cared.

I saw a couple emerge from the shelter in what must have been my darkest hour. I hadn't seen them going inside the shelter and didn't know where they came from. But it doesn't matter. The woman carried a white sheet with her. She laid the sheet over me and Destiny with tears in her eyes and the couple left. I saw a kind heart and some goodness and these strangers were the kiss of an angel, a true blessing.

Beautiful!

When the shelter doors opened at night, the staff was cold and unfriendly. They condemned us for not being Christians, offering no sympathy. I knew we were homeless, but it didn't mean I didn't know God. I knew God and I saw them as heartless, merciless people. That wasn't my belief of what Christian behavior should look like.

I saw other single mothers like me with little children at the shelter. Many of them had also been through domestic violence. I saw for myself that domestic violence often causes homelessness. We were all the remnants of cold and evil men, perhaps people.

We were the broken pieces without the mended tools. We were boxed into shelters to protect us from harm. Yet we were in our own prison where we needed to escape, to find our true self.

I moved from the homeless shelter in Kansas City after staying a few weeks. I moved back to St. Joseph where I used to live and stayed with a friend I met in beauty school.

While I lived with my friend we had sharp disagreements about Destiny because she was a hyperactive toddler. I tried to keep up with Destiny and the criticism of my friend to ease the situation. It was difficult away from a home of my own, and I was uncomfortable. Yet for the moment, I was stuck in her home until better opportunities presented themselves.

I had lived with my friend for a month when I got a phone call from Darlene. She told me she had left the Amish and was living in Wisconsin. I wanted to see her now that she left the Amish and I needed to be with her so I could have a chance to start over. I decided to pack my belongings and move to Wisconsin.

I traveled to Wisconsin on a greyhound bus. I was able to bring baby Destiny on my hip and two large pieces of luggage. I moved to a small town, called Millie Port where resources were as limited as the little town. Yet I got to see my youngest sister again.

With the lack of resources presenting in my new environment, I began to wish for things that were impossible. I wished for a better education which I couldn't have now. There was no college nearby. I also wished to live farther from the Amish now that I had left them. In Wisconsin, I lived right by them.

I often felt lost and like I didn't belong there. Many days I also thought about Isaiah and wished we could've worked things out. Yet I knew his problems were far too troubling for me to fix.

I was living in Wisconsin for a week when I got a job working in a factory. I sewed life jackets all day making a beginner's wage. I didn't find it to be a bad job, and better yet, I got some solitude at my sewing machine.

Things changed as time passed. My boss was not ignoring me as much as she did at first. She started yelling at me whenever it was convenient. It kept getting worse as time went on. I hit the edge of pure anger one day after too much yelling and stormed away from my job. As quickly as this job started, it ended.

I wrote what I was feeling while I lived in Wisconsin. This is what I wrote,

Dear Journal,

"I see snow falling outside. I see myself in a community that I hate with all my breath. I work jobs I hate. I see my dreams, hopes, goals, and desires and I see how impossible it looks to reach them."

I hope that things are never as hopeless as they look-that somehow a golden hue lies beyond the dark gray one. Perhaps the snowflakes that glisten in the sun are glitter fairies just waiting to bring good luck. More-so I can close my eyes and envision a lovely summer day in the forest and as I look up at the sky I see the leaves on the trees. No, they are not leaves but they are money dangling there. The prettiest of all is when it rains and the sun comes out before the rain dries the leaves on the trees, they look like specks of emeralds. If I could roll up into a nutshell and live among the trees-I'd be happy, forever and ever.

Always, Regina

Reality was that I didn't live in a tree but I was living in a tiny apartment with Darlene, me and Destiny at this time. I thought it was cute, but Darlene thought it was too small for all of us. She arranged for us to move to a house out in the country. The house was filthy and ugly, but I found it livable with a little fixing up and a lot of cleaning. So we didn't have to pay a deposit to move into the house. We cleaned and scrubbed until it was livable, and then we moved in.

The house looked cold and oppressing, with a picture of a skeleton hanging on the ceiling in an upstairs bedroom. Old, black material hung over the windows in one bedroom. It was tacked on in the corners of the window and a hole gaped open here and there. An evil-looking cat machine dominated the dining room. I couldn't help it that the possessed looking cats with the stare-y eyes gawked everywhere. There was still unopened beer left in the refrigerator.

On top of that, things began to break mysteriously in the house. The TV broke without warning, and then the microwave literally spun itself and broke. Then other appliances began to break when I was alone in the house. It seemed that everything broke for no reason. It was a cycle of spin, clunk, and stop.

This bothered me so much that I had elders come to the house to pray over it, which actually helped bring a calm atmosphere over the house. We didn't have ugly mysteries happening in the house after that. The breaking stopped.

We lived in an ugly house and I began to understand what my dream meant about living in an ugly house. I knew this was the house represented in my dream. I knew I would get to move to the place which I would choose myself someday. I began to look forward to my future.

Time passed by after I quit my job at the factory. I got another job after a long and tense period and became an activities assistant in a nursing home. I liked this job very much, and the wages increased measurably greater than my previous jobs. I also got the education and license to be a Certified Nursing Aid. I worked hard to accomplish what I had lost in Kansas City.

I started working in every department in the nursing home. I would go to work and ask which department they wanted me to work in. I mostly worked in activities and sometimes as a CNA.

I often finished the day working in laundry. Sometimes I washed dishes in the kitchen and served food and sometimes I worked in housekeeping. I was doing anything and it was just another day at work.

I started college once more to get a degree. I would drive an hour to a nearby town to the college and back home at the end of the day. It was very overwhelming with my job.

I started going to college full-time and finally gave up, cutting out two classes. I then started working full-time and ended up working part-time. Eventually, I got laid off and began receiving unemployment.

I tried to care for my hyperactive little girl while going to college. Yet by no means did I pass my first semester in flying colors. I bumbled through it in pure exhaustion and was completely relieved when it was over. It brought no success, and this lack of success became my worry.

Yet I bought a car from Darlene and learned how to drive. This gave me more independence and encouraged me to keep on trying.

So I packed up my things and moved to a trailer park nearby. I thought the trailer was too dark and the forest behind the house looked spooky. Yet I stayed there because I was with an agency that would help me move to Colorado Springs.

I then went through a period of fasting, prayer, and resting. I also started volunteering in the community food pantry and in a nursing home. I needed solitude and took the time to have that solitude. I started opening my communications and my meditations to God. I believed God told me that I would move someday.

Church people treated me as if I was wrong for caring. Yet I ignored them and focused on God while continuing to pursue my own goals and beliefs. I was dreaming of a better life and I no longer needed their control. I had to believe that life was better than their prayers. I needed hope and courage after my previous experiences with homelessness.

I had a long talk with a wonderful friend. She prophesied about the most wonderful things that would come into my life. It gave me courage in everything I now believed in.

She was a very unforgettable woman and she believed in me. It was now that I began realizing I still had a reason to believe in destiny and that there was a time and season for everything.

I sat on her porch on a sunny day and we chatted together. We went out and pulled the clothes from the clothes line. We sipped on tea and she brought a resiliency into my heart that never left.

I finally started working in another nursing home as a Certified Nurse Aid. I had a certain dread and dislike for this job and all its hard work, but it wasn't all bad. For the first time in my life I saw elderly people cared for in great comfort, and that gave me comfort as well.

It was a Mennonite nursing home with Mennonite staff and patients. Some Amish patients and staff worked there as well. Many non-Amish Christians of different kinds lived and worked there, only Christians.

They still had delicious, home-cooked meals and said blessings before each meal. It was a wealthy nursing home and the patients were ladies and gentlemen. They were people of honor with money and respect.

Sometimes these patients had no appreciation or kindness for the wealth of care they received. They complained about things that patients in other nursing homes would've appreciated.

Nonetheless, the nursing home was a beautiful upper class nursing home with pretty rooms for the patients and staff, and I appreciated and admired that. It lived on the edge of a small town in the prettiest countryside.

I found myself presented with different opportunities to experience life with the Amish again. After all, I was in a nursing home with them, working alongside them.

I had a chance to empathize with a Mennonite girl who worked in the nursing home and wore the prettiest white dresses. She told me about events of sexual abuse when she was a child. I had empathy for her while recognizing a wrong.

I encouraged a young Amish girl to leave the Amish. She wore pretty pink dresses and clearly didn't embrace the rules of the religion. She was happy to listen to me about my life away from the Amish. We thus became good friends.

I listened to a young Amish girl who dressed plain but not neat and dismissed the cape, the extra garment worn over the blouse. She told me all about the hurt she endured in the Amish school when others made fun of her. It made me feel better to listen and try to help as I remembered how heartless school kids could be.

I worked hard for a few months in this nursing home and saved enough money to move to Colorado Springs. The property owners encouraged me to move. They thought I would never have the chance to move again.

Some people thought I would never make it in Colorado Springs, but they were wrong. Not only did I make it in Colorado, but I thrived.

The first thing I wanted to work on accomplishing was finishing beauty school from where it had ended in the face of domestic violence. Now I had a chance to finish my degree and I would work hard on that as soon as I moved.

Consequences of Action

THE FIRST NIGHT I moved to Colorado Springs I was twenty five years old and I had a dream. It went like this:

Once upon a time a man and two women lived in an old house. The main room where they stayed was a bedroom with a plain wooden dresser and a plain bed. The window in the bedroom held no curtains and faced north toward a river running along-side it.

The other rooms in the house weren't used because they were torn up. The ceilings dripped water and the doors didn't lock. The floors were made of plain torn tile and were bare. So everyone stayed in the bedroom as the only safe room in the house.

The man and two women were dressed in simple clothes. They appeared as poor peasant people from an ancient time and were among the poorest people in history. They owned nothing and needed to risk much for what they could get.

They needed money and in a moment of sheer luck they won money. It came like a lottery winning of an unusual sort and became the envy of evil men.

I heard the man say, "It's a miracle. One day we're poor and the next day we're rich".

He held up millions of dollars in his hand and he looked so happy. I couldn't see how they got the money, but they did. I could see the amazement in their eyes.

I also saw fear succumb them in a fashion not seen before the winning. They feared the safety of their own lives.

Suddenly, there was a commotion outside. The man and two women ran to the window and looked outside to see what was going on. They saw scary men trying to reach them to take away their money.

The men were riding on horseback along the river and were trying to cross the river to get to them, but they were unsuccessful.

Then I saw the man and women running through the woods with large black capes blowing in the wind behind them, carrying satchels of money. They were terrified and trying to escape from the scary men.

Again, I saw them back in the house just as in the beginning. They were looking out the window and watching the last man who wanted to rob them fell in the river and drowns. The man and two women were safe again.

I heard the man say, "It's a miracle, our life changed overnight".

I woke up wondering what this dream meant. Surely it appeared as if my dreams communicated with me. Maybe it could mean that someday my life would get better than it was now. I hoped this was true. Although I far from anticipated becoming a millionaire, it was too unrealistic.

I worked hard as a student in beauty school after I settled into Colorado and at the same time I got a job as a certified nurse aid. I was determined to prosper and thrive in my new environment and set out to do so.

I also needed to overcome dark events in my life which I had never truly dealt with. With this fact presenting itself, I had yet another dream.

I looked across a valley to see a land full of beautiful green grass. It was a peaceful place with creeks and brooks nearby. Trees outlined the skirt of the valley and a sidewalk ran through it. It looked somewhat like a scenic golf course that rested alone in solitude.

I looked around and saw an elderly man. He appeared from nowhere and sat down on the sidewalk next to me. He looked at me and said, "You keep doing the same bad things over and over and God is shutting you out. He can't hear you now".

I looked at the old man and I cried out, "I can't stop, I can't stop, and I don't know what to do anymore."

He looked at me and said, "You are staying here where you won't be bothered by anyone. Here is a place for you to be alone and dedicate yourself to God because you don't know him." He stayed nearby as if watching over me, protecting me and watching me heal.

I awoke from this dream, and I knew that a day would come when my addictions would come to an end. A time of refuge lay somewhere out in the world before me. The cycle of events always unfolded itself and brought a different course that taught me lessons.

Of course I didn't know that this turn in events would begin with Alice. She was a chunky, large girl. Her character was that of a careless freak. She didn't care who she hurt and if I asked her to describe herself, she'd reply,

"I'm a crazy drug addict, nymphomaniac with an anger control issue."

She was all of those but she was also hilarious and did many humorous acts. Most of the comments she made were funny which made the work place fun. We were team workers and since she and I were regular co workers' working with each other, I had to associate with her a lot.

Nonetheless I never saw the glory in working myself into a state of exhaustion until I met Alice. You see, I was watching TV one night with Alice at work during a quiet "down" time when she looked at me and asked me casually, "Do you enjoy being a Certified Nurse Aid?"

I answered unconsciously, as usual, "Sure, its okay."

Alice looked at me in disbelief and said, "No Regina, serious, I hate being a shit wiper, come on, don't you want a break from it?"

I answered unemotionally, "Well, I never thought about that."

She said, "I know you're taught to be polite and to say good things about your job to protect it, but you need not with me, because I hate my job."

I replied, "Well it's tough."

She said, "Think about it, you could be stuck doing this for the rest of your life. Now, don't you feel stuck, I do"?

She finished by saying, "Get a grip, Regina, we are stuck with a depressing life, and we don't make much money".

I had never thought about that before. I had been relieved to have a job after an extended period of looking for work. Work was definitely better than crying myself to sleep from lack of money. It's not that we were the worst paid people, but then again we were far from the best paid either.

Yet I knew that I worked too hard, and my life needed an opportunity for improvement. More so, I was working and going to beauty school, which was an overload. I started feeling that I was really stuck without better opportunities and Alice was right; I didn't have a way out.

Alice implemented the idea to me that overtime was fun and produced the desired income. Overtime also produced exhaustion and had to be compensated with drugs and alcohol to bring relief from the burden it caused.

I never thought of doing this before, but I remembered the euphoria of past drug usage. I thought that if this were the only escape I got, I should decide to take it.

We found forbidden territory to hide out, and work became an endless party and a miserable excuse to act out from exhaustion. We slept if we got that lucky, which was rare.

We shopped and ate out while visiting the bars and clubs and getting high. We'd take handfuls of diet pills so we could stay awake for the night shift. We burned out from long extensions of sheer adrenaline.

I graduated beauty school during this time and focused my attention all the more on work. I saw a chance to make more money at my current job rather than to start a new career.

The nice part was that I never had to worry about bills. They were paid and we had money left to eat out and buy whatever we wanted. We bought clothes whenever we wanted but we still lived from paycheck to paycheck, usually because I blew every dime I earned.

Destiny and I lived in a tiny apartment and drove a used vehicle. Some people may have thought we were the squalor of poverty, but I can say that our physical and monetary needs were met. I made sure of that and even went out a few nights with Alice to prostitute for more money.

Prostitution is a sore subject for me. I didn't enjoy any of the men I was with, and it stole my spirit. It is a part of me that is better left unsaid. I had too many miserable dates, too many unstable times. I prostituted for business "money" and business only. Than I quit doing it.

I got what I wanted whenever I wanted. I saw a world full of crooks who "ripped off" people. I decided that since people were conniving and dishonest, I should steal to make sure I got my fair share of the deal.

Alice would say, "The Bible says that people have what they need if they help themselves."

So we helped ourselves. I knew we were wrong, but I was so exhausted and in my exhaustion, I didn't care.

One time after getting high on crystal meth, I went out and stayed in my car for days to recover. Jake, Alice's husband, took care of Destiny while I stayed in the car.

I watched the sky fade in front of me, hour after hour. My mind was fuzz and the night faded into 'shadow people' that appeared everywhere. I finally had Alice drive me home.

It was at home that I realized I was weak and dizzy and couldn't remember my phone number, and then I forgot my address. I dialed 911 when I realized I was beyond functioning and something was wrong, very wrong.

It was a September day when an ambulance rushed me to the hospital. There were needles in me. Someone had me hooked up to a heart monitor. I was breathing through an oxygen machine. I was disoriented and hallucinating. I was a mess and felt like I was dying.

Despite all this drama, I didn't want to believe the hospital staff when they reported I had methamphetamines in my system. I even made them recheck the evidence later, just to make sure.

I had never been in trouble like this before and I couldn't accept the fact that I was in trouble now. I knew I needed that change. Nonetheless it frightened me.

The hospital staff called social services and social service women evaluated me. I signed papers that had me ordered for drug treatment. The evaluation papers said that I had drug-induced hallucinations. I had a mixture of methamphetamines, diet pills, and alcohol in my system.

My fast-paced drug life finally caught up with me, and I found myself to be unmanageable. More so, the lack of my dignity as a result of my drug problem brought out shortcomings in my personality. I forgot my goals while I chased my current problems, and that was the end of living and the beginning of survival.

I had long and difficult months in front of me. Now I saw myself in situations of drug treatment that locked me in jail. I was standing in front of a judge every week and social services took my daughter away from me.

I woke up every morning wondering if my life had come to a brutal end. The thought was absolutely terrifying.

I fell apart when my little girl went to foster care. I had evolved my life around her, and now she was gone. I had my home because my daughter needed a home. I had worked a job to support my daughter, giving me purpose, and now it was gone. I realized I needed to look for a happier path.

I went to court-ordered drug treatment and counseling. I relapsed at times and had my stay in jail. I despaired and quit my job while leaving the influence of drug dealers like Alice and went through another financial struggle.

How fickle and meaningless my life became after it turned sour. Poverty alone created a victim in me without the presence of abuse. It stole my soul and my conscience. I know now that Alice was wrong when she told me I had no way out. I had many paths I could've taken, but I chose not to take them.

Now I started a new life and got a new job. I had to do that while I searched for something better. I also found a new home and saw the return of my daughter. It was through this difficulty that I learned more success and began to see solutions through all my problems.

I changed my attitude toward people and became more caring. I took care of my patients while looking to comfort and reassure them, looking to protect them and keeping them safe. I began the task of changing from bad to good.

One of the most miraculous things happened in Colorado. A nice lady paid off my car. I don't know her name and I never actually knew her. But I shall never forget her for being an angel in a time of need. She handed me a check worth more than a thousand dollars. My car was completely paid. I believed it was a token of blessing for a deed I had performed earlier in my life.

I had given a single parent a car before I moved to Colorado, because I had no longer needed the car. She had left her abusive husband earlier. Understanding abuse and realizing her desperate need for transportation to her job, I decided to help her. It was the right thing to do, and it helped make up for some wrong I did. My efforts were blessed.

I believe now that the God of our universe exists. I believe that God created us as spiritual beings and that spirituality is essential for personal maturity and growth. I also believe that when I practiced love, kindness, and charity I was usually more content.

I believe our faith in God is the most powerful tool we have. It certainly helps shape the purpose in which we are called to live. I always knew that I would work to no end for a new, improved life.

* * *

My drug recovery happened all in one year. It happened along with a judge that I liked. Since she had my respect I was cooperative with her. I was with a local outpatient drug treatment. Although I wasn't fond of any of that treatment, I graduated from it so I could go on with my life, regaining normalcy. Along the way I did a few annoying things to irritate them just for fun. I did a month of inpatient treatment and although it was lonely to me, I did enjoy the benefits of meditation.

I became great friends with the foster family whom were very supportive. We became good friends and this made it so much easier to have a relationship with my daughter. The reuniting with her was much easier because of it. I felt that I got some help that I had been literally, in a sense, begging for. Along the side of these people it was possible to stop using drugs. Above all it helped that I wasn't with Alice anymore. Remember, I had quit that job. I wouldn't enjoy company with her now.

The people I enjoy now are people from good neighborhoods who live the life of a comfortable, respectful citizen. All of us, whom I associate with, we have a future.

I learned happiness a year after I graduated drug treatment. I learned that life isn't always happy. It has good and bad moments. I was just thinking and living different. I realized one thing and that was that if I was to live a satisfied life without the use of drugs, I had to create satisfaction for myself. I got a better job and made goals that inspired me. That helps tremendously.

Dear Journal,

I'm learning something new now and that is that the non-Amish people can be down right mean also. Yet I have seen some good people too. I just have to look past the bad to see the good.

I wonder why I couldn't just look past the bad to see the good when I was still Amish. I suppose I could, Journal, if I didn't believe the Amish were such hypocrites.

Anyhow, my life sure has not been all roses since I have left the Amish. I have done so many troubling things that it's a shame.

I won't always have a life like this though, Journal. I can improve, I'm certain. Now I have more opportunities around me.

Dear me, Life can be so sad at times, but I still look around for those moments of joy. Little things like the night sky glittering with stars, and the sun shining into my kitchen window remind me of good times.

I remember when Mom used to go to the garden early in the morning when the sun came out.

She would pick tea from the garden, spearmint and peppermint leaves. She would put the tea leaves in seeping hot water, in the round glass pitchers.

The sun would shine in from the East and shine into those glass pitchers and it looked so pretty. We would sip tea while we shelled fresh peas from the garden. Those were good mornings.

I still have those moments, even today. I need them to give me small moments of pleasure and peace.

I've discovered that life is made of small moments of happiness. I make as many of those small moments that I can and enjoy them.

Sometimes those moments tend to be nice and long, especially as I pay more attention to them.

I still take the time to smell the roses and fill the vases with them. I make sure I still gaze at the mountains and smell the fresh air. Now and again

I'll pick up an old book and read it from start to finish and watch the sunset until it gets dark.

I can gaze at the mountains here in Colorado and realize that they are beautiful. I live close to the prettiest country there is. We have moose and bears and lots of deer. The historical sites are breathtaking and the air is still as fresh as ever.

Journal, the non-Amish people are no better than the Amish after all, but I'm thankful that I can report abuse without getting shunned and I'm glad that I can still enjoy a crisp clear morning. It is as cozy as it has ever been.

Most thoughtfully and thankfully I say, "Life is good."

Regina

Change of Thoughts

I CAN'T SAY much about the men I dated. I will always remember Isaiah because he gave me something precious, a baby. I cared more for him than any woman ever has, though he was certainly not my true love. His drugs possessed him more than he possessed me. His separation was my broken family and was sorrow in my heart. It was knowledge that something could be beautiful but it was not. It was another broken dream.

All the other men in my life came and went. None of them left strings attached. They were superficial, selfish beings while expecting much and giving little. They brought entertainment for a night and were a tale told and forgotten. They were part of the American preoccupation with what we call casual sex. It lives on in dynamic proportions and offers nothing significant.

I learned that sex is over-valued, over-discussed, over-used, and provides no lasting comfort. It lies out there with the message of over-importance. Yet I discovered that life can be very meaningful without sex.

I needed a respectful man who would actually be useful in my life. I found no such being and therefore had to let them go. I quickly lost interest and shipped them from my mind to planet, sick.

I realized that my prostitution had only made an object out of me. I was proud of my womanhood, and I wouldn't insult it. I worked on my celibacy, education, and efforts for improvement, which brought me comfort.

I take my dreams that I dreamt in the night to point out the obvious. I had rather odd dreams in my sleep. My dreams were always leading me somewhere and showing me where I was going. One dream led me to a place I needed to go for drug recovery.

Many nightmares revealed my destroyed relationship with my father. Many dreams showed me things that would happen and usually did happen later in life. It was as if a dream always forewarned me of future events. In one such dream, I dreamt about the end of the world.

I saw the end of the world approaching. People were running around frantically. There was an aura of panic over everyone. All around me people were rushing and looking worried. Eyes and pattering feet were everywhere, and they didn't stop

I saw an underground tunnel where people were hiding. I saw everyone running from room to room inside the tunnel. There was a look of terror on everyone's faces.

They were trying to escape the world. They believed that God would not find them if they would hide underneath the earth. According to them God only wanted the people on the earth and not beneath the earth. Yet their expressions were fearful.

I saw myself having to make a decision about God. I had to face God with my life face to face. I could not run or hide. I made a decision to face God. At first I felt a little fearful, but then I felt at peace. I believed that everything was going to be well.

With this dream in my mind I noticed that in both worlds, the Amish and non Amish, neither offers a particular goodness or particular happiness. Both worlds have good and bad people and both worlds have the contented and un-contented. There are sad moments and many happy moments. We are, all of us, very human, despite any religion.

I also noticed that many who claimed to be sober and drug-free appeared to have an unfulfilled life. Many of them had quit using drugs but they had lost their jobs, homes, and children. Rather than fighting to get their life back, they simply seemed to accept the fact that they were sober. They proclaimed depression as a disability and lived a desolate life with everything they had lost. It had to be miserable.

Like many other people, I was taught everything about codependency, addictive behavior, the steps of recovery in narcotics anonymous, self-esteem, anger management, relaxation, meditation, and more. They are wonderful subjects and topics that everyone should be taught, but these were things I was taught long before I ever used street drugs.

If you remember that I loved to read and that I learned much from reading, then you may realize that I had already read about many psychological aspects before treatment occurred.

It isn't a bad thing to go through treatment and once more be reminded of all those things, but in the end, I used a healthy thought process I learned from reading books to overcome my drug addiction.

I trained myself to live each moment thinking happy thoughts to replace the bad ones. I'm telling myself all the good, decent things I can do to replace the bad things. I taught myself to look out for the best interest of others and still keep my own interest enacted and protected. It is a good lesson for me

Because of this I can tell anyone that a victim isn't attractive and living in squalor isn't noble or good. Living in peace, without chaos or worry is the quiet solitude that creates happiness.

In the end, the only admiration I had was for people who fought back regaining everything they lost. I was one of them that fought for a respectful life. I simply believed that sobriety was a lost cause if I couldn't regain what was taken when it was lost. I made up my mind and I was unstoppable. I had to un-bend everything that twisted in my life and I did.

I also went back to college and earned another license and I still will continue to do more of this. I have contented myself with a good job and will continue to improve my career, bringing more joy to my life.

Years ago I'm thinking, "I want to get high, I have no way out, this is my escape," Today I think, "I have a life, all my dreams, a future doing something I love. Love and happiness will replace my sadness and bad behavior. Now I have given myself a reason to stay sober.

My Valued Life and Restoration

IT WAS A Christmas in the country with my family. We were all in Iowa at Aunt Nancy's large house. All Amish and non-Amish family were gathered together. I was with my family, having a good time, eating lunch, and then washing dishes. Everyone moved to the living room to converse but Darlene and I stayed in the kitchen.

We wore dresses the way that Mom wanted us to and made sure we wore pretty make-up. We wanted to look neat and pretty for her. We were all singing Christmas songs together, and when I looked out of the kitchen window I could see a cow. He lived across the yard in a pasture with a wooden fence. America was thriving and the countryside was lovely.

Mom was also celebrating her birthday, and we were all giving her birthday cards. I watched Mom open one; it was from Darlene and me. Mom wanted money in her birthday card, and I knew there was no money.

I wanted Mom to have the money so I ran to the kitchen to tell Darlene. Darlene gave me the money and I put it inside the birthday card.

As I walked back to Mom, I realized that something was terribly wrong with her. I ran into the living room to find her lying on the floor. People were applying emergency resuscitation to her. I could see that she was dying. I looked down at Mom and held her feeble hand.

I heard her say, "I love you. You're my favorite child." I held her hand tighter.

I heard one of the emergency workers say, "Blow air into your mother."

I leaned over to do resuscitation on Mom, but eventually I realized that she was gone. I lay next to her, weeping and holding her hand.

I woke from my dream, and in a moment I realized that she was still alive. I shuddered at the dream about her death. I loved her and I didn't want her to go.

Over the years Mom has warmed up to me a lot. She has made up for her lack of affection in my childhood by hugging me every time I've visited (something Amish people don't do). I think she accepts me now.

I am proud of her for taking care of the family financially when Dad did not. She did all her housewife duties and also fulfilled most of Dad's. She ran a business and took care of ten babies. In the end, Mom's wonderful meals and hard-core business mind saved us all. While no one else in the family gives her credit for that much, well Mother, I do.

I am proud of her for not shunning me outwardly and having a pleasant meal with me, despite our differences. I am proud of her for allowing me to be a lady with a pretty dress, hair, and make-up.

I don't envy my mother. She worked too hard and was too tired. I wouldn't want to live her life in which she is forever submissive to her husband and the *Ordnung,* never having the freedom of choice. It may not be so bad being an Amish man, making all of the decisions. It is difficult, though, being an Amish woman.

My relationship with Dad doesn't exist. Aside from a cordial "Hello," we have no ties. It doesn't bother me because we never truly had ties, and I've learned to let go. I forgive him for shunning me. After all it's just part of his religion. He doesn't know better.

As for the harsh discipline in which he raised me, well that's just the Amish way. I don't waste my time worrying or even thinking about it. I have gone on with my life and it's good just the way it is.

My one last, living grandparent died a few years ago. Our entire family, except Ray, attended the funeral. At the funeral I saw how our family has changed. Many of them had been to counseling to seek inner healing. They appeared to accept me, and I realized then that I didn't dread my family anymore.

Time and age has brought reconciliation through healing. Everything good I've done made life complete and it's a wonderful feeling. In regard to a life that has become better and will continue to improve, I had yet another dream.

The ocean rose up on the outskirts of the forest beautiful, but quiet. A ripple didn't stir the water but the sun shone gloriously upon it. The trees stood proud and the grass stood trim. The gazebo rose up with its pretty trellis, yellow roses growing through it.

I saw the beauty of scenery all around me and marveled at it. The weather was perfect in every way and I lived in perfect harmony with my surroundings. I felt perfectly safe and secure and at complete relaxed peace. A large, white dove flew from the heavens and guarded the doorway to this place where no one could enter.

Suddenly, the sky turned dark and cloudy and I saw a dark and gloomy ocean. The water began to toll and rush violently. It looked freezing cold, frightening, and dangerous. Any precautious person would not get close to the ocean because it looked threatening. It seemed to shout a warning to me.

I fearlessly leaped into the ocean. The water was deep, incredibly deep. It seemed like I had plunged into danger. Yet I had an irresistible urge to plunge into the deep. I had to experience the adventure.

I didn't feel anything as I sank through the water. I remember very little of that experience. I remember what I saw at the bottom of the ocean. The ocean floor had jewels, beautiful jewels. They sparkled, glittered, and shone everywhere. I had a powerful urge to collect the jewels. It was an irresistible fantasy, and I reached out to the beautiful, shining jewels. Suddenly I woke up. I saw a beautiful destiny and a dream, a fantasy and piece of happiness. It can exist.

CPSIA information can be obtained at www.ICGtesting.com
Printed in the USA
LVOW081959200312

273986LV00003B/93/P